❖

THE
Stretch & Sew®
GUIDE TO SEWING ON KNITS

❖

THE

Stretch & Sew®
GUIDE TO SEWING ON KNITS

ANN PERSON

Chilton Book Company

Radnor, Pennsylvania

Published in Radnor, Pennsylvania 19089, by Chilton Book
Company

For the *Stretch & Sew* dealer nearest you or for mail-order
information, call 1-800-547-7717 or write P.O. Box 185,
Eugene, Oregon 97440.

The following trademark terms appear in this book: French
Trim, Lycra, and *Stretch & Sew*.

Designed by Rosalyn Carson

Manufactured in the United States of America

Library of Congress Cataloging-in-Publication Data

Person, Ann.
    The stretch and sew guide to sewing on knits / Ann Person
        p.   cm.
    Includes index.
    ISBN 0–8019–8593–5
    1. Sewing. 2. Stretch woven fabrics. I. Title.
TT715.P47   1994
646.4—dc20   94-18469
                                        CIP

1 2 3 4 5 6 7 8 9 0   3 2 1 0 9 8 7 6 5 4

CONTENTS

FOREWORD

❖

Ann Person's approach to knits has always made terrific sewing and fashion sense. She created her own timesaving rules for handling stretch fabrics, all the while taking advantage of the magical knit fit and construction forgiveness. She also designed clothes that were, above all, wearable: flattering, comfortable and classic, no matter what your size.

If you haven't already discovered her special brand of knit sewing, get ready for an exciting sewing experience. I once worked for Ann, and was introduced to her techniques during "Basic Eight" classes taken by all employees. To this day, I remember how terrific the ribbing on my teal-blue top looked—so professional, fast, and easy to do. I also made my first swimsuit—the great fit and quick elastic application were amazing.

Ann and her knowledgeable *Stretch & Sew* staff continue to fine-tune and build their knit-sewing repertoire, compiled conveniently for this book. Can't recollect how to neatly miter a ribbed V-neckline? Insert the no-side-seam pockets? Sew a rugby front tab and collar? Apply lace to a slip or camisole? The answers are all here.

You and I now have a comprehensive guide, complete with the clear, easy-to-decipher illustrations synonymous with *Stretch & Sew* publications and patterns. Oh yes—and you don't have to own a serger to use the book (although helpful tips are provided); how-tos are described and drawn utilizing basic machine stitches.

Bring on the knits—real-life fabrics for real lifestyles and figures—and Ann Person's real-life knit-sewing philosophy. As she says so well, "... you will feel as though you've been set free."

Gail Brown

Gail Brown
Author, *The New Creative Serging Illustrated, Gail Brown's All-New Instant Interiors, Quick Napkin Creations, Innovative Serging* and *Innovative Sewing*

INTRODUCTION

S ewing with knitted fabrics is the essence of this book. What are knits, how do they differ from woven fabrics, and what do you do differently when you sew with them? These are the questions that we will answer for you.

The fact that knits stretch is part of the mystique of the fabric, and as you learn how to use that stretch to your advantage you will be thrilled with the simple and easy results. Just as knits are fun and satisfying to sew, they are also comfortable and lovely to wear. Comfortable because of the "give" in the garment, yet they lack that unwanted bulk often associated with a woven garment.

Once you have mastered a few simple techniques for sewing with these forgiving fabrics, you will feel that you have been set free. Free to sew in a way that was not available to you when you worked with standard woven fabrics, which often were so unforgiving.

To go along with these fast and easy techniques, you will need great-fitting patterns to sew. I have developed a line of patterns that not only fit well but are easy to work with. *Stretch & Sew* patterns are available through your favorite fabric store. Choose a *Stretch & Sew* pattern for each of your garments, from lingerie to tops and pants, and have a great time sewing with knits!

Love, Ann

OTHER BOOKS AVAILABLE FROM CHILTON

❖

ROBBIE FANNING, SERIES EDITOR
CONTEMPORARY QUILTING

Appliqué the Ann Boyce Way

Barbara Johannah's Crystal Piecing

Contemporary Quilting Techniques, by Pat Cairns

Fast Patch, by Anita Hallock

Fourteen Easy Baby Quilts, by Margaret Dittman

Machine-Quilted Jackets, Vests, and Coats, by Nancy Moore

Pictorial Quilts, by Carolyn Vosburg Hall

Precision Pieced Quilts Using the Foundation Method, by Jane Hall and Dixie Haywood

Quick-Quilted Home Decor with Your Bernina, by Jackie Dodson

Quick-Quilted Home Decor with Your Sewing Machine, by Jackie Dodson

The Quilter's Guide to Rotary Cutting, by Donna Poster

Quilts by the Slice, by Beckie Olson

Scrap Quilts Using Fast Patch, by Anita Hallock

Speed-Cut Quilts, by Donna Poster

Stitch 'n' Quilt, by Kathleen Eaton

Super Simple Quilts, by Kathleen Eaton

Teach Yourself Machine Piecing and Quilting, by Debra Wagner

Three-Dimensional Appliqué, by Jodie Davis

CRAFT KALEIDOSCOPE

Creating and Crafting Dolls, by Eloise Piper and Mary Dilligan

Fabric Painting Made Easy, by Nancy Ward

How to Make Cloth Books for Children, by Anne Pellowski

Jane Asher's Costume Book

Quick and Easy Ways with Ribbon, by Ceci Johnson

Learn Bearmaking, by Judi Maddigan

Soft Toys for Babies, by Judi Maddigan

Stamping Made Easy, by Nancy Ward

Too Hot To Handle? Potholders and How to Make Them, by Doris L. Hoover

CREATIVE MACHINE ARTS

ABCs of Serging, by Tammy Young and Lori Bottom

The Button Lover's Book, by Marilyn Green

Claire Shaeffer's Fabric Sewing Guide

The Complete Book of Machine Embroidery, by Robbie and Tony Fanning

Creative Nurseries Illustrated, by Debra Terry and Juli Plooster

Distinctive Serger Gifts and Crafts, by Naomi Baker and Tammy Young

The Fabric Lover's Scrapbook, by Margaret Dittman

Friendship Quilts by Hand and Machine, by Carolyn Vosburg Hall

Gail Brown's All-New Instant Interiors

❖

Gifts Galore, by Jane Warnick and Jackie Dodson

Hold It! How to Sew Bags, Totes, Duffels, Pouches, and More, by Nancy Restuccia

How to Make Soft Jewelry, by Jackie Dodson

Innovative Serging, by Gail Brown and Tammy Young

Innovative Sewing, by Gail Brown and Tammy Young

The New Creative Serging Illustrated, by Pati Palmer, Gail Brown, and Sue Green

Owner's Guide to Sewing Machines, Sergers, and Knitting Machines, by Gale Grigg Hazen

Petite Pizzazz, by Barb Griffin

Putting on the Glitz, by Sandra L. Hatch and Ann Boyce

Quick Napkin Creations, by Gail Brown

Second Stitches: Recycle as You Sew, by Susan Parker

Serge a Simple Project, by Tammy Young and Naomi Baker

Sew Any Patch Pocket, by Claire Shaeffer

Sew Any Set-In Pocket, by Claire Shaeffer

Sew Sensational Gifts, by Naomi Baker and Tammy Young

Sew, Serge, Press, by Jan Saunders

Sewing and Collecting Vintage Fashions, by Eileen MacIntosh

Simply Serge Any Fabric, by Naomi Baker and Tammy Young

Singer Instructions for Art Embroidery and Lace Work

Soft Gardens: Make Flowers with Your Sewing Machine, by Yvonne Perez-Collins

Twenty Easy Machine-Made Rugs, by Jackie Dodson

KNOW YOUR SEWING MACHINE, BY JACKIE DODSON

Know Your Bernina, second edition

Know Your Brother, with Jane Warnick

Know Your Elna, with Carol Ahles

Know Your New Home, with Judi Cull and Vicki Lyn Hastings

Know Your Pfaff, with Audrey Griese

Know Your Sewing Machine

Know Your Singer

Know Your Viking, with Jan Saunders

Know Your White, with Jan Saunders

KNOW YOUR SERGER SERIES, BY TAMMY YOUNG AND NAOMI BAKER

Know Your baby lock

Know Your Pfaff Hobbylock

Know Your Serger

Know Your White Superlock

STAR WEAR

Embellishments, by Linda Fry Kenzle

Make It Your Own, by Lori Bottom and Ronda Chaney

Sweatshirts with Style, by Mary Mulari

TEACH YOURSELF TO SEW BETTER, BY JAN SAUNDERS

A Step-by-Step Guide to Your Bernina

A Step-by-Step Guide to Your New Home

A Step-by-Step Guide to Your Sewing Machine

A Step-by-Step Guide to Your Viking

1 GETTING STARTED

❖

Selecting Fabric

As you examine knit fabrics, you'll learn the fundamental properties to help you achieve the results you want in your garment. Important to the finished appearance are the weight and "hand" of the fabric. How does it feel when you hold it? Firm? Soft? Light? Textured? Smooth? Select a fabric that will lend itself to the look you wish to achieve with your chosen pattern.

What to Look For

You'll discover an array of fabric types available, from single knits, jerseys, interlocks, sweaterings and double knits—and the list goes on and on.

The most important quality to look for when choosing a knit is good recovery. That means when you pull on the fabric horizontally (across the bolt) it will snap back quickly into the original position. If it stays stretched out, or if it returns *very* slowly, any garment you make from the fabric will sag, bag, or "grow" as you wear it.

The amount of stretch in the fabric will determine what kind and size of pattern you will want to choose. Stretch is also important to the way the garment will feel when you wear it. Fiber content and the stitch of the fabric also will affect the final appearance and feel of the garment.

The combination of these factors—recovery, amount of stretch, fiber content, and stitch—will determine how your garment fits.

Differences in Fabrics

The following describes some of the most popular knit fabrics you'll be using to create the wearables in this book.

Single Knit

You can recognize a single-knit fabric because the right and wrong sides appear different. Also, the cut edges of a single-knit curl to the right side of the fabric when pulled on horizontally. When pulled vertically, they roll to wrong side. Single knits are often referred to as "jerseys."

Single knits can be knit from any fiber. Some of the nicest single knits are made of 100-percent cotton. They tend to have a little more body than the blends. The disadvantage of 100-percent cotton is that it must be pressed after it is removed from the dryer. Fabric that is 100-percent cotton usually shrinks more in the washer and dryer than a blend. A common blend is a combination of cotton and polyester. Polyester adds durability and shape retention to the fabric to keep your garment looking new through many washings. Polyester also resists wrinkles. Wool is also used in single-knit constructions. Single knits are drapable and sew well into garments such as pullovers as well as into dresses with soft drape. They have about 25-percent stretch.

Double Knit

Some of the nicest knit fabrics to work with are double knits. A double knit is just as it implies: two beds of needles work in unison to create a fabric that in most cases appears the same on both sides.

❖

Double knit has nice elasticity, varying from 25 percent to 75 percent or more, depending on the fibers and the stitch used. The most common stitches on a double-knit machine would be a Piqué, Ponte de Roma, or Jersey stitch. One advantage of a double knit is that it lies flat, which makes pressing open seams while making a garment much easier.

A double-knit fabric will have more body than a single knit and for this reason it is usually used for dresses, jackets, pants, and coats. Again, the fibers used in knitting double will vary. Wool is one of the loveliest of the double-knits, cotton is used in sportswear and summer garments, and acrylics are often used individually or blended with other fibers, such as cotton or wool.

Interlock

The difference between an interlock and a single knit is that an interlock fabric is really a double knit, knit with fine yarns. Like a double knit, it won't roll as you work with the fabric. An interlock fabric does not have a right or wrong side. Both sides are the same. The stitch appears much the same as a single knit on the right side, although usually it is finer.

The main difference between the interlock stitch and a single knit or double knit is the amount of stretch. The stretch in interlock is more like that of a rib knit. The average amount of stretch in an interlock is 50 percent.

Sweaterings

Heavier yarns and crimped and textured yarns are often used in sweaterings, giving them the wonderful loft and hand we all love. The fibers can vary from cotton and acrylic to wool and blends. Because the yarns are heavier (two- or three-ply), the fabric and stitch have more bulk or body.

The stitches used in sweaterings are usually single knit, but some are made on a double-knit flat-bed machine. When a sweater fabric is knit on a flat-bed machine, the edge at the bottom will be finished and will not need to be finished any further. Fabric knit on a circular machine, whether it is single or double knit, will be a continuous piece that has to be cut to size and then finished on the bottom edge.

Ribbing

Ribbing, as the name implies, is a series of knit and purl stitches. Most ribs are made from a knit one/purl one stitch. Yet there are rib fabrics that will have a variation, such as knit two/purl two. The rib stitch has more stretch than any other stitch—as much as 100 percent. The nicest rib fabrics are knit from cotton, wool, and cotton/polyester blends. Sometimes a Lycra fiber will be added to provide more stretch and recovery. The right and wrong side of a rib stitch will appear the same.

Ribs are used for neckbands, cuffs, and hem finishes. Some ribbed collars, cuffs, and hem finishes on the market have a finished edge on the bottom, making it simple to finish a neck or hem. Otherwise ribbing is knit on a tubular machine that produces a continuous rib. This fabric must be cut and folded so that the folded edge will be the finished edge.

Velour and Terry

A single-knit construction is used to produce velours and other pile fabrics. Pile fabrics can be cut or left in a loop. Sometimes they are brushed to create other effects. Because they are single knit, the amount of stretch is usually about 25 percent, but again that can vary. The fibers are usually very fine in a velour and a little heavier or coarser in a terry.

Pile fabrics are usually made of cotton or cotton/polyester blends, but some nylon pile fabrics are used to make robes. Knitted pile fabrics are most often used in sportswear and loungewear.

❖

Sweatshirt Fleece

Sweatshirt fleece is actually a terry variation. For the napped look, the terry loops are clipped and then the surface is brushed. This gives a smooth fabric surface on one side and a fleece-like napped surface on the other. Sweatshirt fleeces are used for all kinds of garments, not just sweatshirts and sweatpants. The fibers used in the nicest sweatshirt fleece are usually cotton or cotton blended with polyester.

Warp Knits

Lingerie fabrics and swim fabrics are knit on a warp-knit machine. "Warp-knit" is a process that is a cross between weaving and knitting.

Power Net Fabric

This warp-knit fabric is used for girdles and bras and has stretch in both directions. To determine crosswise grain and lengthwise grain, use this method: When you stretch the power net in one direction, the holes will open; this is the lengthwise grain. When you stretch the power net the other direction, the holes close; this is the crosswise grain, or the fabric's greater stretch direction. Power net is made from nylon yarns and has excellent stretch and recovery.

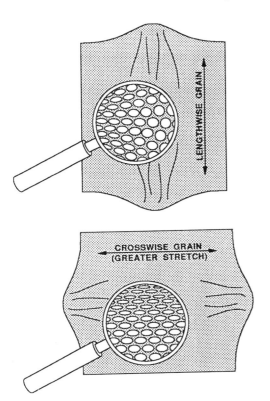

Tricot

Lingerie fabric for slips and panties is usually made from tricot fabric. As with other lingerie fabrics, the fibers in tricot are usually nylon. The fabric is smooth and silky, with a good amount of cross-wise stretch, usually 25 to 35 percent. Some tricots are specially treated with an anti-cling agent that is nice for slips.

Swim Fabric

Swim fabric is a nylon knit with a Lycra yarn added for strength and greater stretch. The percentage of Lycra in a swim fabric will determine the amount of stretch. Swim fabrics, because of the Lycra and the warp stitch, will stretch both up and down or lengthwise as well as across. The most stretch on a swim fabric will be lengthwise. This is because the warp threads contain the greater amount of Lycra.

Exercise Fabric

Most exercise fabric is sewn from a single knit fabric that is made from cotton and Lycra yarn. The cotton gives the fabric breathability, making it comfortable to work out in, and the Lycra gives the fabric bounce and good stretch. Because these fabrics are single knits, the greater stretch is across the fabric; but because of the Lycra, there is also good up-and-down stretch. These fabric usually shrink a lot, so be sure to preshrink before cutting your garment.

Working with Patterns

The timesaving techniques in this book can be used with any pattern. Be sure to check the seam-allowance widths of your pattern against those used in the techniques included here. Some adjustments may be necessary.

Taking Your Measurements

The first step in preparing your pattern is to take your body measurements. You will then be able to determine your pattern size and find out whether or not you must make any pattern adjustments to ensure a good fit.

It's easier to take your own measurements if you work with a friend because it is sometimes difficult to measure your own body accurately. As you measure, hold the tape snug to the body, but not too tight. You should be able to feel the tape against your body, but it should be loose enough to slide back and forth easily.

Here are some tips for obtaining accurate measurements:

- Take your measurements at least twice to ensure accuracy.

- Stand up tall, assuming your normal posture.

- Stand with your feet slightly apart.

- Wear a comfortable, fairly new bra in the style you most often wear.

- Wear shoes with your preferred heel height. Don't stand barefoot, as your figure will take on slightly different proportions.

- To determine your natural waistline, tie a piece of string around your waist. Bend slightly from side to side and the string will settle naturally at the waistline indentation.

- As you take your measurements, record them along with the date you took them. Whenever you suspect you've gained or lost weight or that your figure has changed in any way, be sure to take your measurements again before beginning a new garment.

Begin by measuring your bust, running the tape around the fullest part of your bustline. Whenever you take around-the-body measurements, keep the tape measure parallel to the floor.

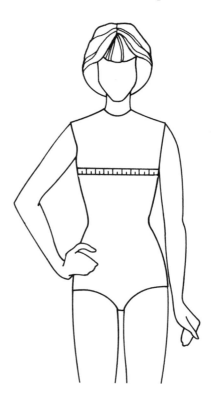

Next, take your waist measurement.

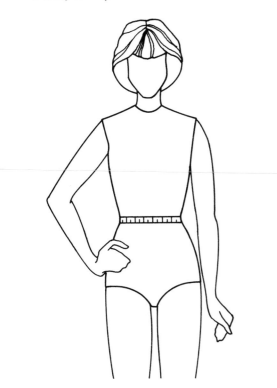

Take your hip measurement by measuring around your body 9″ (23.0 cm) below your waistline, or at the fullest part of your hip.

❖ Your back shoulder width is the distance across your back from shoulder bone to shoulder bone. Locate your shoulder bone by swinging your arm back and forth to feel the point of movement at the joint.

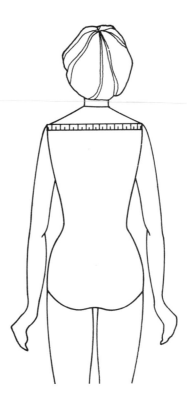

To take your center back waist-length measurement, start at the cervical bone (the most prominent bone at the base of your neck), and measure down the length of your back to your waistline, as shown on the next page.

❖

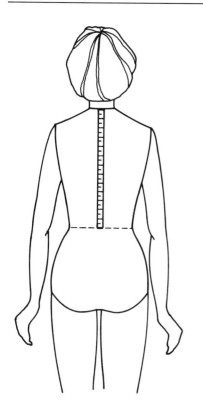

Measure your upper arm approximately 1″ (2.5 cm) below where the arm joins the body. With your elbow slightly bent, take your arm-length measurement, starting at your shoulder bone and measuring over the bend of the elbow to your wrist bone.

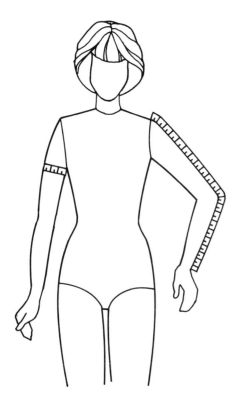

Tailoring a *Stretch & Sew* Pattern to Size

Stretch & Sew patterns are tested for use with both knit and woven fabrics. Some designs, however, are best sewn only from knit fabrics to assure a better fit. Such information is usually listed on the back of the pattern envelope.

Stretch & Sew patterns are designed as "master patterns." Each pattern includes a range of sizes. This enables you to create a pattern that fits your figure, either by using one standard size or by combining several sizes to arrive at just the right fit for you.

❖❖❖❖❖

O ur customers like the idea of a well-fitting pattern in multiple sizing and that they can change sizes, since no one is a perfect size. I am also pleased that the majority of Stretch & Sew patterns can be used on wovens, as well as knits.

MARY CAEN
STRETCH & SEW
LA MESA, CA

❖❖❖

The size range for each pattern is indicated on the front of the envelope along with "views" of the garments featured in the pattern. The back of the envelope includes a yardage chart, a listing of notions required, and the recommended fabrics for the pattern—all the information and items you need to leave your sewing center prepared to sew.

On the back of the envelope you will also find the *Stretch & Sew* Standard Body Measurement Chart.

❖

STRETCH & SEW STANDARD BODY MEASUREMENT CHART

Inches									
Size	30	32	34	36	38	40	42	44	46
Bust	30	32	34	36	38	40	42	44	46
Waist	22	24	26	28	30	32	34	36	38
Hip (9" below waist)	32	34	36	38	40	42	44	46	48
Back Shoulder Width	14	$14^{1}/_2$	15	$15^{1}/_2$	16	$16^{3}/_8$	$16^{3}/_4$	$17^{1}/_8$	$17^{1}/_2$
Center Back Waist-Length	$15^{1}/_2$	$15^{3}/_4$	16	$16^{1}/_4$	$16^{1}/_2$	$16^{3}/_4$	17	$17^{1}/_4$	$17^{1}/_2$
Arm Length	$22^{3}/_8$	$22^{1}/_2$	$22^{5}/_8$	$22^{3}/_4$	$22^{7}/_8$	23	$23^{1}/_8$	$23^{1}/_4$	$23^{3}/_8$
Upper Arm	$9^{1}/_2$	10	$10^{1}/_2$	11	$11^{1}/_2$	12	$12^{5}/_8$	$13^{1}/_4$	$13^{7}/_8$

Centimeters									
Size	30	32	34	36	38	40	42	44	46
Bust	76.0	81.0	87.0	92.0	97.0	102.0	107.0	112.0	117.0
Waist	56.0	61.0	66.0	71.0	76.0	81.0	87.0	92.0	97.0
Hip (23.0 cm below waist)	81.0	87.0	92.0	97.0	102.0	107.0	112.0	117.0	122.0
Back Shoulder Width	35.5	37.0	38.0	39.5	40.5	41.5	42.5	43.5	44.5
Center Back Waist-Length	39.5	40.0	40.5	41.5	42.0	42.5	43.0	44.0	44.5
Arm Length	57.0	57.0	57.5	58.0	58.0	58.5	58.5	59.0	59.5
Upper Arm	24.0	25.0	26.5	28.0	29.0	30.5	32.0	33.5	35.0

It is so easy to get a great fit with a *Stretch & Sew* pattern because the pattern includes all the sizes on a master sheet. You can select the correct size for yourself at *each* part of your body. So if you don't fit *one* size exactly, you don't have to guess how much to increase or decrease if you're not an exact size.

Stretch & Sew patterns are designed according to the *actual* measurements on the envelope measurement chart. The proper ease has been included for each design, allowing you to choose your size by your exact measurement.

Start by comparing your measurements to those on the chart on page 7. Circle yours and see where you most closely fall.

Start with your bust measurement. Our example has a 36″ bust. Trace the 36 through the bust.

The example has a 40″ hip. That hip measurement belongs to a size 38 pattern. Gradually taper from the size 36 at the bust to a size 38 at the hip.

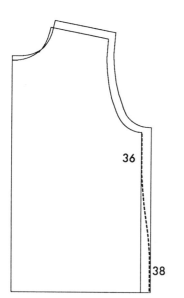

The back shoulder width in the example is 15″. That corresponds to a size 34, so gradually taper to a size 34 at the shoulder, keeping the size 36 along the shoulder edge for height. A size adjustment will not be necessary for the sleeve.

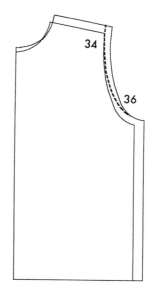

If your measurements fall in between the measurements on the chart, such as a 37″ bust, just cut or trace in between the sizes 36 and 38 for your pattern. Use a different colored marking pen or pencil so you can easily see your customized pattern lines.

Also, you may want to make adjustments to the finished garment length. To determine your desired finished length for dresses or tops, measure from the cervical bone at the back of your neck to the desired hemline.

❖

For skirts, measure from your center back waistline to the desired hemline. For pants, measure the outseam from your waist to the desired hemline. Then compare this measurement with the finished garment length shown in the chart on the back of the pattern envelope. The difference between your desired finished length and the finished length on the chart is the amount you will need to adjust for your pattern length. Use this same procedure to check sleeve length.

Pattern Fit and the Fabric's Percent of Stretch

Always be aware of the stretch of your fabric and how it will work with the pattern you have chosen.

Knit fabrics have degrees of stretch that affect the fit of the garment.

The method for determining the percentage of stretch in knit fabrics is simple. Fold your fabric on the crossgrain approximately 12" (30.5 cm) from one cut edge. Place 10" (25.4 cm) of the *fold* along the first 10" (25.4 cm) of your tape measure.

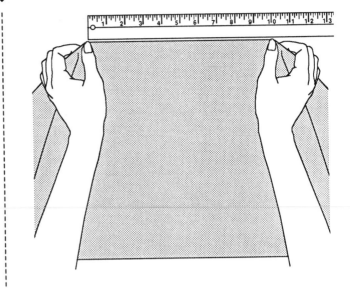

Hold the fabric in place at the left end of the tape. With your right hand, pull the fabric past the 10" (25.4 cm) mark as far as it will comfortably go. If the fabric will stretch *easily* to 12½" (31.8 cm), you have 25-percent stretch. If it stretches to only 11" (27.9 cm), you have less than 25-percent stretch. If it stretches to 15" (38.1 cm), you have 50-percent stretch.

There should be some stretch left in the fabric. If you can stretch a piece of fabric easily to show 25-percent stretch, you can usually force it to show 35-percent.

DETERMINING PERCENT OF STRETCH

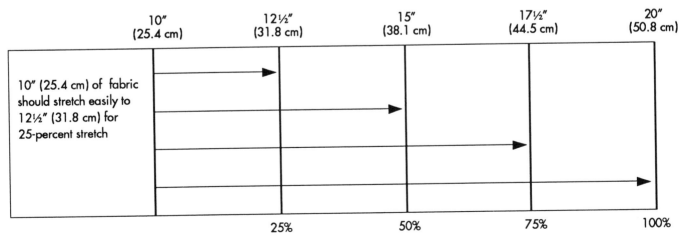

10" (25.4 cm) of fabric should stretch easily to 12½" (31.8 cm) for 25-percent stretch

10" (25.4 cm)	12½" (31.8 cm)	15" (38.1 cm)	17½" (44.5 cm)	20" (50.8 cm)
	25%	50%	75%	100%

Check the back of your pattern envelope for suggested fabrics. Most *Stretch & Sew* patterns are designed to be used with woven or knit fabrics with up to 25-percent stretch. If your fabric has 50-percent stretch, cut or trace your pattern one size smaller than your regular size. The greater stretch of the fabric allows enough ease in the garment to create a good fit from the smaller pattern size.

If your pattern is designed for fabrics with only 25-percent stretch and you choose a less stretchy fabric, you may wish to adjust your sizing, especially if the design is close-fitting.

Laying Out and Cutting the Pattern

Before beginning your pattern layout, you'll want to determine the fabric's lengthwise grain, right and wrong sides, and greater stretch—all important guidelines for making an accurate pattern layout.

Make pattern layout and cutting easy by using pattern weights. They secure the pattern and eliminate the need for pinning. The fabric won't slide off the table either.

STRAIGHT-OF-GRAIN

You'll want to determine the lengthwise grain of the fabric. The lengthwise grain runs the length of the fabric, or parallel to the selvage. Each pattern piece has a line labeled "Straight-of-Grain." Lay the pattern pieces on the fabric so that the straight-of-grain line aligns with the lengthwise grain of the fabric.

GREATER STRETCH

When sewing with knit fabrics, you'll also want to determine the direction of the fabric's "greater stretch." When you gently stretch the fabric, you'll see that there is more give in one direction than in the other. Usually the greater stretch runs crosswise. In most cases, you will place the pattern pieces on the fabric so that the greater amount of stretch goes *across* the pattern, or *around* the body in the finished garment. This will provide you with a comfortable fit.

Of course there are exceptions to every rule. When working with a border design, for instance, you may want to ignore the stretch or selvage rule to create a special effect.

Swimwear fabrics usually have the greater amount of stretch knit in the lengthwise grain of the fabric. In this case, when cutting out a swimsuit, refold your fabric so that the greater stretch will go *around* the body.

MARKING THE FABRIC'S "RIGHT SIDE"

Some fabrics, such as interlock and double knits, have a right and wrong side that look much the same. If both sides look identical, it doesn't matter which side you choose for the right side. But it is important to use the same side for the right side throughout your garment because there may be a slight difference you do not detect. Use a pin or strip of transparent tape to mark the right side.

SPECIAL LAYOUT CONCERNS

Nap

Before you cut your pattern pieces, notice whether your fabric has a nap or a one-way design. In some fabrics you can see but not feel the nap by observing the way the light reflects off of them. Other fabrics have a nap you can see *and* feel. To determine the nap direction, run your hand down the length of the fabric. If it feels smooth, the nap is running down. If it feels rough, the nap is running up.

❖

Cutting napped fabrics like velour with the nap running *up* each garment piece will enhance the richness and depth of the fabric's color. Always be careful to lay all the pattern pieces in a single direction on napped fabric and on fabric that has a one-way design.

Some napped fabrics, such as chenille, shag terry and fun fur, have a long nap which falls in one direction. Cut these fabrics with the nap running down.

Deknitting

The term "deknitting" refers to the fabric coming un-knit or running. This most often occurs on fabrics that are knit from a very slick yarn. The raw or crosswise cut is the edge that can deknit. By gently pulling on the cut edge of the fabric, you can determine whether the yarns are going to have a tendency to deknit or run.

Most knit fabrics are processed to prevent deknitting. Occasionally, however, a nylon or polyester fabric with a very silky appearance may have a tendency to deknit if stress is applied to the cut edge. If you pull the cut edges, you'll see that the fabric deknits from one edge only. When positioning pattern pieces on such a fabric, place them so that the fabric's deknitting or "running" edge is at the *lower edge* or hemline of the garment, where there is less stress.

Fabrics That Twist

Cotton jersey is knit on a circular knitting machine, and once the fabric is washed and dried it may twist a bit. In this case, ignore the selvage rule and place your pattern pieces as illustrated.

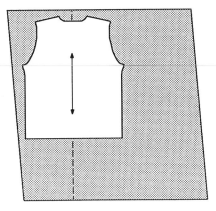

Center Crease

One final consideration is the crease that runs down the center of some knit fabrics. This crease may have been permanently set by the manufacturer in the fabric finishing process. The permanent crease will occur when the fabric has been processed while it is still in a tube, whether it was knit that way or whether it has been slit and then sewn back together to match the stripes. To determine if the crease is permanent, try to press it out. If you cannot, you'll want to position your pattern pieces either to avoid the crease entirely or make sure the crease runs down the center of the sleeve, but never down the center front or center back of the garment.

MATCHING STRIPES

To match stripes on your pattern, you must cut your pieces one at a time from a single thickness of fabric. If your pattern is for only half a Front and half a Back, you will need to redraw the pattern onto tracing material in order to have a full Front and Back pattern piece with which to work. Do this by placing the center front and center back of the pattern on the fold of your tracing material, just as you would on the fold of your fabric, and cut it out so you now have a full Front and a full Back pattern piece.

When cutting a top, first cut one Back, making sure each underarm point is on the same stripe. Use the Back as a guide for cutting the Front, matching all the stripes. You may find it helpful to fold the pattern down at armscye to make sure you have placed it along the same stripe. Now cut one Sleeve, placing the underarm points on the same stripe you placed the underarm points of the Front and Back.

Use the first Sleeve as a pattern for the second Sleeve, matching the stripes exactly. Remember to turn the sleeve over before cutting the second piece so that you have a right side and a left side of the garment.

If you are using cotton jersey, ignore the straight-of-grain and make sure your stripes are straight on your garment.

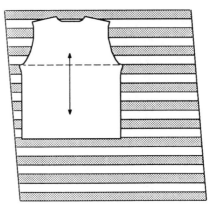

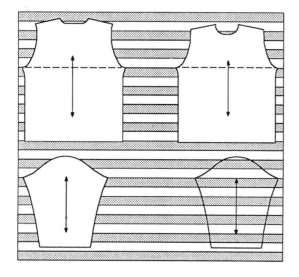

❖

MARKING THE PATTERN

Transfer all construction markings to your fabric and interfacing. It's a good idea to note the size and length you're cutting or tracing and the date. Then, after a period of time, it's easy to know whether to cut or trace a new pattern to adjust for a weight change or a length change. You might also want to note the fabric you're using.

CUTTING TECHNIQUES

The most common question when I start a new class or talk to a customer in a store is, "But if I cut it, won't it run?" The answer is "*no*, it will not run." Sweater bodies and knit yardage have been processed and in this processing the yarn has matted, eliminating the chances of it running when it is cut. Even the very loose knits are perfectly safe to cut. In fact, to try to extract a raveling to mend a slight flaw is no small chore.

Do not cut knits with pinking shears because the fabric edges will shred.

Cut the garment pieces from your fabric, referring to the suggested cutting layouts in the pattern instructions and the Special Layout Concerns explained on pages 10–12. If your fabric doesn't have an obvious right and wrong side, mark the right side for each piece as you cut it using a pin or a strip of tranparent tape.

To ensure strong seams, cut notches outward rather than clipping into seam allowances.

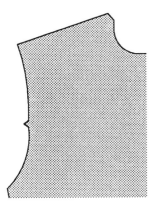

Getting Ready to Sew

Supplies

PINS

Long glasshead pins are excellent to use when sewing knits. They have round, white glass heads and extra-long shafts which makes them easy to see and use; they won't slip through the yarns on soft, knitted fabrics. Always remember to remove pins as you sew. Sewing over pins may break or blunt your machine needle and may damage your fabric.

BASTING TAPE AND GLUE STICK

Basting tape, which is adhesive on both sides, is a great substitute for pins when positioning trim, laces, and zippers prior to stitching. After stitching, simply lift off the tape to remove it. The tape comes on a roll and is ⅛" (0.3 cm) wide.

A glue stick is nontoxic and water-soluble, so it washes out. It is easy and convenient to use on both fabric and paper.

THREAD

The old rule for choosing thread was to match the thread fiber to the fabric fiber: polyester on polyester, cotton on cotton, silk on silk. Today's fabrics are likely to be a blend of fibers such as polyester and cotton or polyester and rayon, so matching the fiber is not important. Most of the *all-purpose* threads on the market are polyester or a cotton-wrapped polyester and are well suited for sewing on all fabrics. Large cones of all-purpose thread are available for use with sergers. When sewing with lightweight fabrics, such as lingerie or lightweight silkies, use an *extra-fine or lingerie* thread.

❖

Specialty threads are fun to use and can add an extra dimension to your garment. Most can be threaded through the loopers of your serger or wound onto the bobbin of your regular sewing machine. *Woolly nylon* is a thread that stretches and so is nice to use on activewear and swimwear because it gives with the garment. Don't use woolly nylon if you will need to press the garment with a hot iron. The thread melts at a low temperature. *Rayon thread* is great for appliqué because it is shiny and makes a pretty satin stitch. Always test your stitch when using a specialty thread because you may need to adjust your tension to accommodate the thicker or coarser thread.

SEWING MACHINE

Any properly maintained and tuned sewing machine will be appropriate for sewing knits, although a machine with a zigzag stitch is particularly useful and allows you more detailing opportunities.

Keep your sewing machine clean and well oiled to ensure skip-free, balanced stitching. Refer to your sewing machine owner's manual for details on the care and service of your particular machine, and have your machine serviced on a regular basis by a qualified sewing machine service shop.

For strong, smooth seams, you'll need to see that the needle tension on your machine is properly balanced. To determine this, straight stitch on a double thickness of scrap fabric in the direction of greatest stretch. When the tension is correctly set, your stitches will be even on both sides of the fabric, with no puckering or loose stitches. A good way to test this balance is to stretch a stitched portion. If both threads break evenly, your stitch is balanced. If only the needle thread breaks, the needle tension is tighter than the bobbin tension. Most manufacturers do not recommend adjusting the bobbin tension. Generally you should adjust the needle tension to match the bobbin tension.

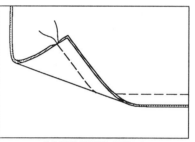

CORRECT TENSION

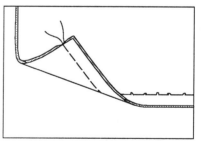

TOP TENSION TOO TIGHT

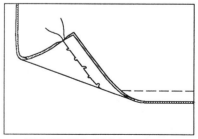

TOP TENSION TOO LOOSE

❖

NEEDLES

Ballpoint or stretch needles are the best for sewing knit fabrics. These needles will penetrate your knit fabrics by sliding between the yarns without damaging or cutting their fibers. A ballpoint needle has a slightly rounded end and works best with heavier-weight double knits, while the stretch needle has a completely rounded tip, which is best for finer-weight knits such as lingerie, interlocks, and swimwear.

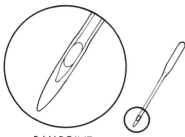

BALLPOINT

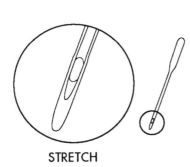

STRETCH

The universal needle has a modified ball point, and works well on both knit and woven fabrics. Because of its shape, it also helps to prevent skipped stitches. This needle is good for general sewing purposes which means you can save time and money because you won't have to stock up on a variety of needle types.

Needles come in a variety of sizes. Sizes 8 to 11 American or 60 to 75 European work best for lighter-weight knits; sizes 12 to 14 American or 60 to 70 European work best for heavier-weight double knits.

Use a new needle as you begin each knit garment. Needles tend to dull when sewing and that can lead to skipped stitches or snagged fabric. And by all means, avoid sewing over pins, thus protecting your needle from becoming bent or dulled. A blunt needle causes a thumping sound as it sews through fabric. Run your finger across the tip of the needle. You may be able to tell easily if your needle is dull. Pull the needle through your fingers and feel for a burr on the end. Even a new needle can be imperfect.

A sure way to detect a blunt needle is to hold the needle point between your fingers and look down the shaft. If it is shiny, the point is blunt. You should not be able to see a sharp needle point.

A bent needle is readily visible and if not replaced can result in skipped stitches, or the needle can strike the throat plate of the machine and break.

Finally, clean your needle from time to time with some rubbing alcohol or a specially formulated sewing product to reduce the buildup of static electricity, which can cause skipped stitches.

❖

Preventing Skipped Stitches

If your sewing machine is skipping stitches, hold the fabric taut to prevent it from clinging to the needle. When the fabric clings to the needle, it holds up the thread so that the hook on the bobbin assembly doesn't pick it up. This causes a skipped stitch.

Check the needle for residue that builds up when you sew with synthetic fabrics and causes the fabric to cling to the needle. Remove the residue by cleaning the needle with rubbing alcohol.

Sometimes when you work with closely knit fabric, your machine may persist in skipping stitches. The general opinion of sewing machine dealers is to use a smaller needle that will have a better chance to penetrate the fabric. I disagree. The reason the machine skips is that the thread is held back by the tight knit. Then the thread is not in the proper position for the hook of the bobbin assembly to pick it up and form the stitch. By using a larger ballpoint or stretch needle with a larger groove, the thread can lie in that groove and not be held back by the fabric so that it can complete the stitch. As I said, this is contradictory to many opinions, but it has worked best for me. So, if you are having a problem, try this method. Instead of going from an 11 (75) needle to a 9 (60), try switching to a 14 (80).

If you are having trouble with skipped stitches, switch from a wide zigzag presser foot to a narrow straight-stitch foot. This will help hold the fabric in place and prevent it from clinging to the needle.

If your machine regularly skips stitches, even on normal double knits, the timing is off, and you should take the machine to your dealer for repair.

Serger

The serger has sold quite well in the last fifteen years in the American market. No invention that I know of has helped the home seamstress in her labors more than a serger. The reason that a serger is so great when sewing with knit fabric is that the seam sewn with a serger has elasticity. The seam will stretch and not break, so stretching as you serge is not necessary. Serging knits keeps the seam allowance nice and flat and eliminates the need for doublestitching. It is not necessary to serge-finish an outer edge of a double-knit seam that will be pressed open, but sewing a ¼" seam with a serger is a real joy.

The question might be, "Do I need a serger to sew with a knit?" and the answer will be "No!" Need and want may be another matter. The serger is important for overcasting a seam when working with a woven fabric that has a tendency to unravel or fray when washed.

Iron

Your steam iron becomes invaluable when sewing with knits. The steam does all the work and the iron itself touches the fabric only lightly.

Pressing is a must for a beautifully finished garment. To sew a seam and not press it before sewing another seam over that area can make the difference between a homemade look and a beautifully finished garment. I save time in pressing by positioning my ironing board so close to my machine that I can swing around in my chair to press a seam without getting up.

The secret of pressing knits is to press without stretching or pulling the fabric. It is vital not to pull your garment out of shape. A neck area or facing can be accidentally stretched when pressing so that the two will not match when sewn together.

❖

It is also important to press your fabric before you cut it out to be sure the knit hasn't closed up during washing and drying. Pressing will assure that the garment doesn't grow as you wear it.

To press effectively without damaging the fabric, use a damp or wet press cloth, which protects the fibers and provides steam to achieve the necessary temperature. The type of press cloth you use is a matter of personal preference as long as it is absorbent. Moisture is necessary to provide adequate steam. I prefer a square of white cotton interlock. For convenience, I keep a bowl of water at my ironing board to use when the cloth needs to be dampened.

A cotton ironing board cover also helps to protect fabric. The cotton absorbs the heat instead of reflecting it. If the heat is reflected back, the temperature may build until it is too hot for your fabric.

Be careful when pressing acrylics. The moment steam hits acrylic fibers, they relax and easily stretch out of shape. So don't let the garment hang over the side of the ironing board or the steamed area will stretch. You should also allow the garment to cool before you move it from the ironing board. Incidentally, you can impart new body to acrylic by pressing with a damp cloth until the cloth is dry.

Pretreating Fabric

At one time or another, you've probably purchased a fantastic pullover, worn it once, washed it—and then it shrank into a short, fat little top! One of the many benefits of making your own clothes is getting the chance to shrink fabric *before* cutting out and sewing the garment. Then you're free to launder the finished garment without having to worry about it losing its shape. You'll also discover that many fabrics look even prettier after they've been washed.

Whatever you plan to do to your garment after you have cut and sewn it, do to your *fabric first*. If you feel there is a chance that you might put the garment in the dryer on hot, even if by mistake, put the fabric in the dryer now. There is nothing more disappointing than working hard to make a lovely garment and then have it shrink so that it no longer fits.

My pretreating rule has always been a simple one: *Before cutting, treat your fabric exactly as you plan to treat it as a finished garment.* Refer to the care instructions on the fabric bolt end for guidelines. For example, if you plan to machine wash and dry the garment, machine wash and dry the uncut fabric at the machine settings you will use for the finished garment.

Remember to use soap in this first washing to remove any excess dye and sizing that could be in the fabric. Using a soap rather than a detergent will help your knits stay bright.

If you plan always to dry clean the garment, pretreating usually isn't necessary. Woolens, however, should be steamed, with the exception of those labeled "needle ready."

It should not be necessary to prewash the fabric more than once. I have heard stories from customers who reported that their fabric continued to shrink in a second and third washing. This is probably because the fabric was not knit and sold at the same width. This doesn't happen often. Some discount manufacturers used to knit the fabric narrow and then steam and stretch it wider for sale. This causes the fabric to shrink with each washing until it reaches its original knitted size.

It is not necessary to pretreat most interfacings you will be using with knits.

❖

One important exception to the pretreatment rule is: *Do not pretreat ribbing that will be used as trim unless you plan to use a dark-color trim on a light-colored garment.* In this case, cut your rib trim the correct length and then soak in a vinegar and water solution to "set" the dye and pretreat. This will help prevent the dark color from running into the garment in subsequent washings. Test the treatment by sewing a test strip of ribbing to a fabric scrap and washing them to be sure the color is set.

Garment Basics

Seams

The seam finish you choose for your garment depends on the fabric.

SEWING A SEAM

At *Stretch & Sew* we have always taught the method of *stretching the seam as you sew* and using a setting of 3. That translates to 9 stitches to the inch. Using the longer stitch and gently stretching the fabric as you sew does not pile a lot of thread in the seam that could make the seam stay stretched or give a ripple effect. Here are the basic stitches used to sew a seam.

Straight Stitch

For some knits you'll want a ⅝″ (1.6 cm) straight-stitched seam and will press it open. This will be nice on double-knits and bulky knits that will stay pressed open well. For knits that roll you may want a ¼″ (0.6 cm) seam. To stretch and sew is as the name implies: I stretch the seam as I sew it. When the seam relaxes to its original size, I have a seam with the same elasticity as my knit material, a seam that will stretch with the fabric. The rule is: *The looser the knit, the longer the stitch; the heavier the fabric, the lighter the pressure.* I do not recommend changing the tension on your

machine because the upper and lower tensions are balanced. If you change only the upper tension, the machine will be unbalanced and the lower thread will be apt to break or pull out.

Instead, stretch the seam slightly as you sew with the longer stitch. When the seam relaxes, the stitches are close together and the tension, both upper and lower, automatically loosens. Stretching the fabric assures the necessary give. This will give the seam the same elasticity that the knit fabric itself has.

For some knits like jerseys and single knits that tend to roll, a ¼″ (0.6 cm) seam works best. Overlocking is not an absolute must with knits, as most knits do not ravel. The main advantage of an overcast seam is the more professional look. You can either doublestitch or serge the seam and press it to one side.

The straight-stitch presser foot is a sewing machine foot, usually metal, specially designed to sew with a straight stitch. I find this foot helpful when I work with a fabric that had a tendency to skip stitches. The smaller opening of the foot helps to hold the fabric taut and keep it from clinging to the needle, which is most often the cause of skipped stitches. This foot is also helpful when working with heavy fabric where the seams are particularly thick.

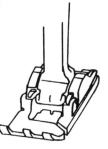

STRAIGHT OR ZIGZAG FOOT

Plain Straight Stitch versus Stretch Straight Stitch

Thirty years ago I worked with a sewing machine company that wanted to promote its unique straight stitch. A special setting on their machine created a stitch that basically went two stitches forward and then one stitch backward.

The disadvantage of the stretch straight stitch is that the multiple stitches have a tendency to oversew the seam, creating a weakness in the fibers from all the needle action.

The method that I taught throughout my career of teaching sewing with knitted fabric was to use a little longer stitch (stitch length setting 3, or 9 stitches to the inch). I still prefer to use the longer stitch and stretch the fabric as I sew. The only time I would use a stretch straight stitch would be to sew the crotch seam on a pair of blue jeans!

Backstitch

Backstitching secures the threads and prevents seams from coming undone. In most cases, backstitch at the beginning of a seamline and then stitch forward over the reverse stitching.

If the seam will be trimmed, backstitch where the seamlines will cross instead of at the beginning of the seam. This way you will not trim away the backstitching.

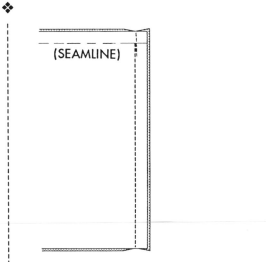

(SEAMLINE)

Double-Stitch

If sewing with a regular sewing machine, doublestitch ¼″ (0.6 cm) seams by sewing a second row of stitching on the seam allowance ⅛″ (0.3 cm) from previous stitching. This helps to keep the seam allowance flat and pressed to one side. It is not necessary to doublestitch seams that will be topstitched.

Zigzag Stitch

Use the zigzag stitch with knits when you want a great deal of stretch. I do not use it to sew a seam, but I would to apply elastic. A rather wide and well-spaced zigzag is best.

The zigzag presser foot is used for most sewing when you have a machine that will zigzag. Thus, even if you are sewing with a straight stitch and wish to use a zigzag occasionally, you are not hampered by that choice.

Years ago I used a multiple zigzag to sew on elastic, but after a number of failed attempts to remove the stitches for correction, I learned that a plain zigzag worked as well and was simpler to remove.

Serging a Seam

Set the stitch length and width on a number suitable for your fabric and adjust the thread tension to produce an overlocking stitch that does not bind or ruffle the seam. Each looper thread should lie smooth on the fabric. Serged seams have some stretch and help keep the seam allowance flat.

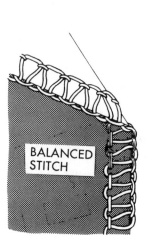

BALANCED STITCH

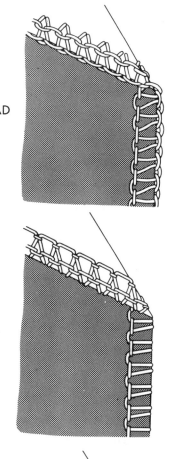

NEEDLE THREAD TOO LOOSE

UPPER LOOPER THREAD TOO LOOSE

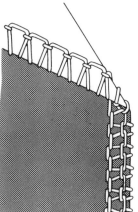

LOWER LOOPER THREAD TOO LOOSE

Some sergers come with a differential feed adjustment. With the differential set on the lower setting, the front feed dog will take shorter strokes than the back feed dog, causing the fabric to stretch slightly as it is sewn. This setting can be used to add additional stretch to activewear or swimwear. With the differential set on the higher setting, the front feed dog will move farther than the back feed dog, causing the fabric to compress or ruffle, in effect easing the fabric. This is a helpful setting when sewing a bias-cut seam or ribbing onto a garment to avoid a wavy seam.

Hems

Straight-Stitched Hem

For a straight hem, press in the hem allowance. Pin the hem in place so the heads of the pins extend beyond the folded edges for easy removal as you stitch. Use a straight stitch and stretch slightly as you sew to build elasticity into the hem. When sewing with striped fabric, select thread that matches one of the stripes and then sew along the edge of the stripe for a nearly invisible hem. Steam-press the hem after stitching to remove any ripples that may have formed.

If you are working on a very stretchy knit fabric, to avoid having the hemline "grow," use a longer stitch length or sew your garment slightly narrower at the hemline before hemming.

FLATTERING V-NECKLINES– EASY ON AND FUN TO APPLY.

A WARDROBE OF BASIC NECKLINES, MADE MORE FLATTERING AND EASIER THAN EVER TO SEW, THE *STRETCH & SEW* WAY.

SECRETS OF THE TRADE—HOW TO TURN A PLAIN NECKLINE INTO A VARIETY OF LOOKS FOR WHATEVER YOU DO AND WHEREVER YOU GO.

A VERSATILE NECKLINE, THE RUGBY CAN BE PART OF ANY LOOK, FROM OFFICE TO PLAY. FOLLOW THE FASHION LEAD—WE'LL SHOW YOU HOW.

❖

BLINDHEM

The blindhem stitch is a good choice for knits because the bulkiness of the knit will hide the stitches well. The blindhem does not have a tendency to stretch the fabric as much as a straight stitch.

A machine-stitched blindhem gives you the look of a hand-stitched hem in a fraction of the time. You'll need a blindhem foot on your machine. Serge or finish the raw edge of the garment as desired. Press the hem in place. Fold the hem back to the right side of the garment, allowing the cut edge to extend approximately ⅜″ (1.0 cm) past the fold. Using the blind-stitch setting on your machine, stitch on the extended hem edge, adjusting the stitch width and length to barely catch the fold on the zigzag stitch. Your stitches should not show on the right side of your garment. Loosening the top tension can help prevent a dimple from showing on the right side.

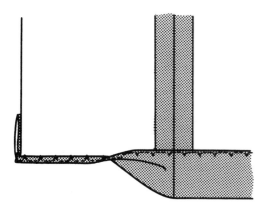

The blindhem presser foot has a piece of metal in the center that forms a guide to help keep your blindhem even. The foot is also helpful when edgestitching.

BLINDHEM FOOT

FUSIBLE WEB HEM

A quick way to hem a garment is to use fusible web. This is a continuous strip of multifilament nylon that melts when heat is applied. I like to use a ⅛″-wide (0.3 cm) strip of the web. If you keep the web narrow, it will be less likely to show the hem on lighter-weight knits. If you have some wider web on hand, just trim it to the width you desire. After pressing in your hem, place the web between the garment and the hem with the edge of the web along the cut edge of the hem. The web will stick to the iron if it is not completely covered with fabric. Bond the hem in position using a steam iron (wool setting) and a damp press cloth. Iron until the press cloth is dry. This will give you a permanent bond that is safe and easy to wash or dry clean.

RIBBED HEM

For a lower-edge rib band, cut a strip of ribbing 6½″ (16.5 cm) wide by two-thirds of the measurement of the garment's lower edge. Add ½″ (1.3 cm) for seam allowances.

Using a ¼″ (0.6 cm) seam allowance, stitch the lower band together to form a circle. Finger-press the seam open.

❖

Fold the trim in half lengthwise with wrong sides together. Divide the trim into fourths and mark with pins.

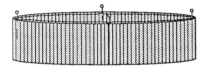

Divide the lower edge of the garment into fourths and mark with pins.

Pin the trim to the garment, matching the quarter divisions, cut edges, and seams.

Using a ¼″ (0.6 cm) seam allowance, stitch with the trim on top, stretching the trim to fit.

DECORATIVE HEMS

There are many decorative stitches you may use for hems.

Double-Needle Stitching

Double or twin needles are two needles placed on a spacer bar. The width of the double needle will vary from 1.6 mm to 6.0 mm. The 4.0 mm is a nice widely spaced needle that will work well on most of the newer machines, whereas the 6.0 mm will work only on machines that are made to handle the additional width. *In order for a machine to sew with a double needle, it must be a zigzag machine* and it must thread from the front.

Set the machine on a regular straight stitch. The needle sews a double row of straight stitches on the right side of the garment, perfectly spaced with no extra care on your part, and creates a zigzag stitch on the wrong side. There is no need to stretch when using a double needle.

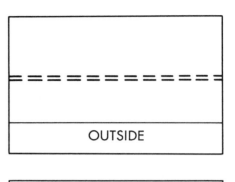

OUTSIDE

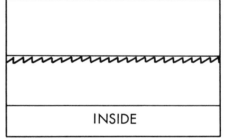

INSIDE

The double needle is very effective when sewing with knits. Because there are two threads in the upper part of the machine, the bobbin makes a zigzag stitch, thus creating a seam that has stretch built in. The double needle is an excellent choice for topstitching a swimsuit after the first application of elastic. When you need more than one row of stitching, the double needle ensures the even division of the stitching.

It is important when sewing with a double needle that you place each thread on opposite sides of the tension disks on the machine. Thread one thread through the thread guide at the top of the needle and bring the second thread straight down to the needle from the take-up lever.

❖

The tension for the double needle will depend on the effect you want to achieve. By having a normal tension on a fairly widely spaced double needle, you will create a slightly raised area between the needle. To allow the fabric to lie flat between the needles, loosen the upper tension until the stitch appears as you wish it to.

Topstitching with a double needle creates a professional-looking finish. The bobbin thread zigzags between the needle threads, which gives the stitch some stretch. Straddle the seamline with the needle and topstitch.

Triple-Needle Stitching

Use a triple needle when you want to add multiple colors of topstitching, each thread a different color. Since most machines do not have three thread holders, wind a bobbin and place it either over or under one of the spools of thread. If your thread holder is not long enough, use a straw, which will give you added length.

Tension disks have only two sides, so it will be necessary to place two of the threads on one side and the third on the opposite side.

CAUTION:

When working with the double or triple needle, do not try to use a zigzag or decorative stitch. The machine is not wide enough to handle the additional width and a broken needle will result.

Buttonholes and Buttons

On knit fabric, the most important thing I can say about machine adjustments is *keep the pressure light*. For a good buttonhole on a knit, make the stitches farther apart than the normal satin stitch used for woven fabrics. This is something you should practice over and over again before actually putting the buttonholes into your garment. If your garment has interfacing underneath where the buttonholes will be stitched, they should go in fairly easily by just using a looser satin stitch. If you are working on a garment that is not interfaced or that has ribbing where you need buttonholes, try one of the methods below for easy application.

Stabilizers

If your knit fabric is not overly stretchy, you can stabilize the buttonhole by pinning strips of fusible web on the top and bottom of the fabric over the buttonhole placement line and then marking your buttonholes on the web. Stitch the buttonholes with a slightly longer stitch length. Tear away as much of the fusible web as you can. Carefully steam the remaining web while holding the iron away from the fabric. Do not touch the iron to the fusible web.

If your fabric is very stretchy, as in a loose ribbing or a stretchy sweater knit, I recommend that you use a heavier tear-away or melt-away stabilizer. The tear-away products look like heavyweight spun-fiber interfacing and tear away easily from your stitches after use. The melt-away products are removed by heating them with an iron and then brushing the residue off. There is even a wash-away product that disappears when water is applied. Whichever product you choose, the technique for using a stabilizer is basically the same. Place a strip of the stabilizer on both the top and bottom of your fabric and mark the buttonhole placement on the stabilizer. Stitch the buttonholes with a looser stitch, then remove the stabilizer by tearing, melting, or washing!

❖

BUTTONHOLES ON RIBBING

When making a buttonhole in ribbing, try to make the buttonhole go with the rib of the fabric rather than across it. This isn't always possible, but you will notice on most sweaters with buttonholes that the buttonhole runs up and down rather than across.

CORDED BUTTONHOLES

Another technique for making buttonholes in a knit is to make a corded buttonhole. The cord can be pulled up to keep the buttonhole the desired size and shape. Consult your sewing machine manual.

When trying to get a thick sweater fabric under the buttonhole foot on your machine, drop the feed dogs until you can position the garment properly. Then be sure to bring the feed dogs back into position before you start to sew.

The buttonhole presser foot has two grooves on the bottom of the foot to allow the two rows of stitching on the buttonhole to pass freely under the foot. Some machines have automatic buttonhole feet as well.

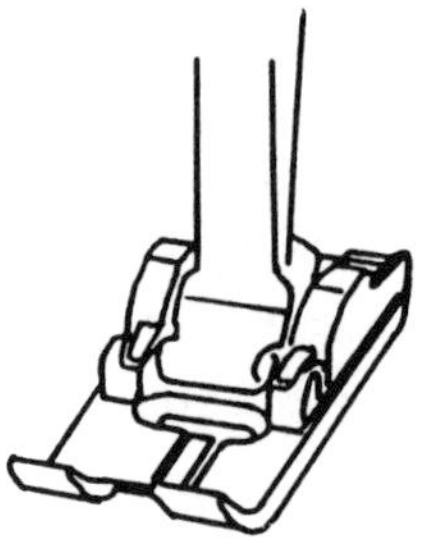

BUTTONHOLE FOOT

2 PULLOVER TEES

A knit pullover is one of the fastest garments you can sew. The edges can be finished with ribbing, so no zippers or button openings are necessary because the knit garment can stretch over your head. Whether you are working on a dress, shirt, or tunic, the construction of the tee is the same: shoulder seams, neckline, sleeves, sides seams, and a finished lower edge. This chapter will give you helpful instructions for each of these components, with special emphasis on the variety of necklines that can top off a tee!

Basic Construction

Sleeves and Side Seams

Pullovers from knit fabrics are best when sewn from a pattern designed for knits. They have a flat sleeve cap and can be applied before the side seam is sewn. This flat sewn-in sleeve is one of the easiest sleeve applications ever devised. And it's simple to match stripes with the body of the garment.

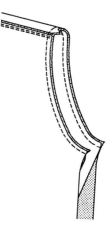

With the garment on top and the Sleeve next to the sewing machine, stitch or serge the armhole seam. Take care to match the stripes.

Stitch or serge the second Sleeve in the same manner as the first. Press the seam allowances toward the Sleeves.

For another great finish, press the seam toward the garment and topstitch it in place.

TAPERED SLEEVES

Tapered sleeves are great in knit fabrics. They can taper to the wrist measurement or slightly smaller for a snug fit, and they are still comfortable when you bend your arm because the knit fabric stretches. If your sleeve pattern is designed for a cuff, you can change it to a tapered sleeve by trimming from the wrist up to the underarm, as illustrated. Be sure to add length at the lower edge to compensate for the missing cuff width and seam allowance. Add a 1″ (2.5 cm) hem allowance.

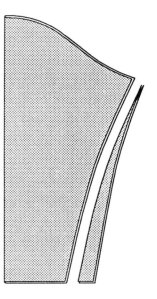

BASIC SLEEVES

This sleeve application works best with ¼″ (0.6 cm) seam allowances. If your pattern has a ⅝″ (1.6 cm) seam allowances, trim the sleeve and armscye to a ¼″ (0.6 cm) seam allowance before you stitch by removing ⅜″ (1.0 cm). With right sides together, pin the Sleeve to the garment at the cap, the underarm points and halfway between the underarm and the Sleeve cap. If you are matching stripes, you will be able to match them only to the halfway point. It isn't possible to match them through the Sleeve cap.

SIDE SEAMS

After sewing in the sleeves, you are ready to stitch or serge the side seams. To sew them, stitch from the lower edge of the garment to the edge of the sleeve, matching underarm seams.

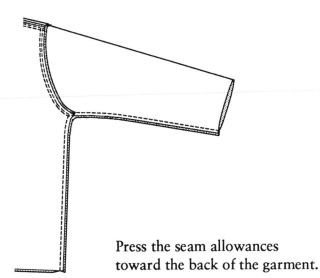

Press the seam allowances toward the back of the garment.

Instructions for serging the side seams (usually done when the cuffs are also serged) are on page 28.

SLEEVE FINISH

If you have tapered your long sleeve or have a short sleeve, you may wish to hem the sleeve. If your sleeve is full, then you will want to add a rib cuff at the lower edge. You can apply the cuffs by sewing or serging them, as explained in the following instructions.

Sewing Rib Cuffs

For a long sleeve, cut two strips of ribbing 5½" (14.0 cm) wide by the wrist measurement *plus* ½" (1.3 cm).

If you are sewing for someone else and cannot measure the wrist, use the following measurements to cut the ribbing.

RIB CUFF MEASUREMENT CHART

Ladies		
Sizes	Inches	Centimeters
30–34	6¾	17.1
36–40	7	17.8
42–46	7½	19.1

Children		
Sizes	Inches	Centimeters
19–21	6¼	15.9
23–25	6½	16.5
27–29	6¾	17.1

For a short sleeve, cut two strips of ribbing 2½" (6.4 cm) wide by the upper arm measurement *minus* ½" (1.3 cm).

Using a ¼" (0.6 cm) seam allowance, stitch each cuff together, forming a circle. Finger-press the seams open.

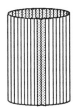

Fold the ribbing in half lengthwise with wrong sides together. Divide the ribbing into fourths and mark with pins.

Divide the lower edge of each Sleeve into fourths and mark with pins.

❖

With the garment wrong side out, pin the ribbing to the garment, matching the quarter divisions, cut edges, and seams.

NOTE:

If the cuff will not stretch to fit the lower edge of the Sleeve, machine baste ⅛" and ⅜" (0.3 and 1.0 cm) from the lower edge of each Sleeve for gathering.

Using a ¼" (0.6 cm) seam allowance, stitch with the ribbing on top, stretching the ribbing to fit and pulling the basting threads to help ease in fullness if necessary.

Serging Rib Cuffs

Rib measurements are for sleeves with ¼" (0.6 cm) seam allowances. If your pattern has ⅝" (1.6 cm) seam allowances, adjest your pattern accordingly.

To cut cuffs for long sleeves, cut one strip of ribbing 5½" (14.0 cm) wide by twice the wrist measurement *plus* 1½" (3.8 cm).

To cut cuffs for short sleeves, cut one strip of ribbing 3½" (8.9 cm) wide by twice the upper arm measurement *plus* 1½" (3.8 cm).

With wrong sides together, fold the cuff ribbing in half lengthwise, matching the cut edges.

For long sleeves, on one end of the ribbing mark the wrist measurement plus ½" (1.3 cm); for short sleeves, mark the upper arm measurement minus ½" (1.3 cm). Mark the second set of wrist or upper arm measurements ½" (1.3 cm) away.

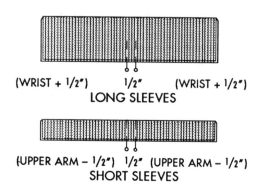

(WRIST + ½")   ½"   (WRIST + ½")
LONG SLEEVES

(UPPER ARM − ½")   ½"   (UPPER ARM − ½")
SHORT SLEEVES

Place one Sleeve under the ribbing, matching the cut edges and secure with the presser foot. Serge, stretching the first mark on the ribbing to match the end of the Sleeve.

Without cutting the ribbing strip, place the second Sleeve under the ribbing at the second set of markings and stitch as above.

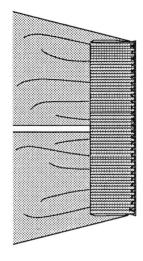

Cut the ribbing between the Sleeves.

SERGING SIDE SEAMS

Serge one side seam from the cuff to the lower edge of the garment using the following procedure.

For a secure cuff, begin serging approximately 2" (5.1 cm) from the end of the ribbing and sew to the cuff edge. Be sure to match the ends of ribbing and to keep the cut edges even while you sew.

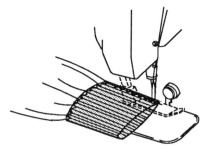

❖

Raise the needle and presser foot. Slightly loosen the needle thread and pull the threads off the prongs. Gently turn the fabric over toward the front so that the underside of the fabric now faces up. Place the cut edge of the fabric next to the knife to avoid loose threads and place the folded edges of the ribbing directly under the needle.

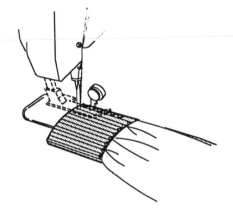

Serge over the previous stitching and continue stitching the side seam to the lower edge of the garment.

Lower-Edge Finish

The hem you choose to finish the bottom edge of your tee will depend on the style of the garment, the pattern instructions, and the fabric you're using. Refer to Hems on pages 20–23 for more information.

Necklines

Applying a ribbing or knit-fabric neckband is one of the most exciting sewing techniques you will ever learn. You can use it on anything from a child's T-shirt to an elegant sweater top for yourself. And you can add it to patterns that call for a different neckline. This chapter provides instructions for only some of the many neckline variations possible.

Crew Necks and Mock Turtlenecks

For a crew or a mock turtleneck, choose a pattern with a natural neckline. The first step is to trim the neck edge of your garment if necessary. This removes the amount you will be adding when you apply the neck trim. Some patterns are designed for ribbing at the neckline and are already trimmed. Check your pattern instructions before cutting away any additional fabric.

❖❖❖❖❖

*M*y favorite patterns are the Stretch & Sew *wardrobe patterns. What would our wardrobes be without them? I like to use them to teach various necklines. I wear outfits made from them in the store and am constantly asked "Did you make that? What pattern are you wearing?"*

I'm pleased that Stretch & Sew *patterns are also for wovens, as well as knits.*

MARY JUDD
FABRICATIONS
KENNETT SQUARE, PA

❖❖❖

❖

Basic Crew Neck or Mock Turtleneck

ADAPTING THE NECK

Fold Front and Back in half, wrong sides together. For ribbing that will be 1¼″ (3.2 cm) wide when finished, trim ¾″ (1.9 cm) from the neckline of patterns with a ¼″ (0.6 cm) seam allowance. Trim 1⅛″ (2.9 cm) away from patterns with a ⅝″ (1.6 cm) seam allowance.

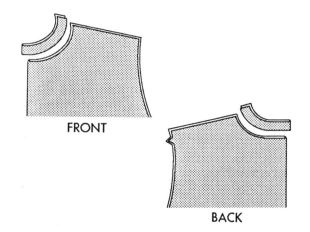

FRONT

BACK

Once you've cut away the neck edge, you will sew the rib trim on with a ¼″ (0.6 cm) seam allowance, regardless of the seam allowance on the rest of the pattern.

CONSTRUCTING SHOULDER SEAMS

Sew the shoulder seams, using the type of stitch you have determined best for your fabric. (See Seams, pages 18–20.)

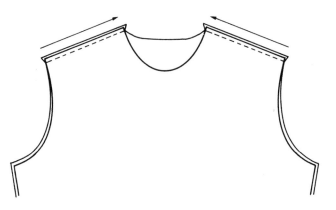

If you are working with a very stretchy fabric, you may want to sew a piece of clear elastic in the seamline to keep the seamline in place but still allow it to stretch. Cut the elastic the same length as the shoulder edge on the pattern piece.

Press the seam allowance toward the back.

A nice touch is to topstitch the shoulder seam. The topstitching holds the seam in place through many washings and it creates a decorative look on the right side of the garment. To topstitch, press the shoulder seam allowances toward the back of the garment and topstitch on the right side, catching the seam allowance on the underside.

MEASURING THE RIBBING

After sewing the shoulder seams, you're ready for the neck rib. Fold the garment in half as illustrated. (You may wish to lay the pattern on the garment to be sure the neck hasn't stretched.)

❖

Standing the tape on its side for accuracy, measure along the ¼″ (0.6 cm) seamline of the neck edge. Double this amount to determine the total neck edge measurement.

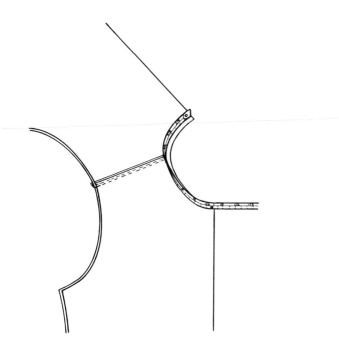

The length of your ribbing strip should be two-thirds the length of the garment neck edge with ½″ (1.3 cm) added for seam allowances. This means you'll apply the rib to the neck edge with a 2:3 ratio—2″ (5.1 cm) of ribbing to 3″ (7.6 cm) of neck edge. As you sew, you will be able to stretch the ribbing to fit the garment neck edge. After stretching, the ribbing will return to its normal length at the natural neckline, providing a close-fitting neckband.

To determine two-thirds of the neck edge measurement, divide the measurement by 3, and then multiply that number by 2. Add ½″ (1.3 cm) for seam allowances.

Another handy way to determine two-thirds of the neck edge is to fold the length of the measurement on the tape into thirds. If, for instance, the measurement is 21″ (53.3 cm), fold the first 21″ (53.3 cm) of the tape as illustrated.

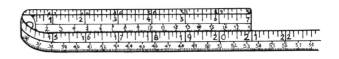

Then unfold the last third and read the tape at the end of the second third. For our example of a 21″ (53.3 cm) neck edge, you will have a reading of 14″ (35.6 cm).

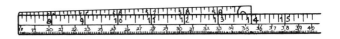

Ribbings vary greatly. For the best neckline results, be sure to choose a rib that has at least 50-percent stretch and excellent recovery.

◄──────── GREATER STRETCH ────────►

CUTTING THE RIBBING

To cut the ribbing for a crew or mock turtleneck, follow the directions below.

For a crew neck, cut the ribbing 3″ (7.6 cm) wide (finished width 1¼″[3.2 cm]) by the ⅔ measurement you just took, plus ½″ (1.3 cm) for seam allowances.

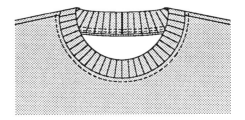

For a mock turtleneck, cut the ribbing 5″ (12.7 cm) wide (finished width 2¼″ [5.7 cm]) by the ⅔ measurement you just took, plus ½″ (1.3 cm) for seam allowances.

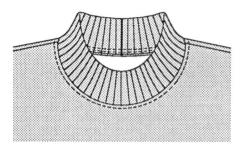

USING KNIT FABRIC INSTEAD OF RIBBING

Some fabrics, like interlock, can be used in place of ribbing at the neck edge, cuffs, and lower edge. The fabric must have at least 50-percent stretch *and* excellent recovery. That means the fabric must bounce right back to its original shape after being stretched.

You apply knit fabric like ribbing. The only difference is you'll need a little longer piece. Use a 3:4 ratio for knit fabric. So, for every 4″ (10.2 cm) of neckline, you'll cut 3″ (7.6 cm) of trim. Remember to add ½″ (1.3 cm) for seam allowances.

APPLYING THE NECK TRIM

To sew the ribbing or knit-fabric trim to the neck, follow these steps:

Using a *¼″ (0.6 cm) seam allowance,* sew the ends of the trim together, forming a circle. Finger-press the seam open.

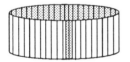

Fold the trim in half lengthwise with wrong sides together. Divide the trim into fourths and mark with pins.

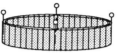

Divide the neck edge of garment into fourths and mark with pins. The quarter marks may not fall at the shoulder seams.

With garment wrong side out, pin the trim to the neck edge, matching the seam in the trim to the center back, quarter divisions, and cut edges.

Using a *¼″ (0.6 cm) seam allowance,* stitch with the trim on top, stretching the trim to fit. Press the seam allowances toward garment.

Topstitch on the garment a scant ¼" (0.6 cm) from the seam, catching the seam allowance on the underside. If you try to stretch this seam as you sew, it may ripple. It does need some give, however, to pull over the head. Holding your fabric flat and smooth as it feeds through the machine, along with the pressure of the presser foot, will give you the ease you need.

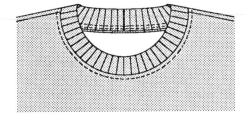

❖❖❖❖❖

*O*ur business was started eight years ago in a 300 square foot store. The first investment we made was a small rack of Stretch & Sew patterns. As we grew, so has our investment in Stretch & Sew. We now have a 7200 square foot store and a complete line of Stretch & Sew. patterns and books. We find we have excellent results with the patterns in our fitting classes.

Thanks, Stretch & Sew, *for helping us to provide our customers with a product we can be proud to have in our store.*

BETTY VOLSKY AND BEV HAAS
BERNINA SEW & SO
DICKINSON, ND

❖❖❖

Crew Neck with Purchased Knit Collar

Make this easy neckline on your next sweatshirt or pullover.

SELECTING A KNIT COLLAR

Use a purchased knit collar at least 3" wide by 15" long (7.6 by 38.1 cm). A purchased knit collar has three finished edges. The edge you sew to the neck is unfinished.

CONSTRUCTING THE GARMENT

Fold the Front and Back in half with wrong sides together. Trim the neck ¾" (1.9 cm) for patterns with a ¼" (0.6 cm) seam allowance. Trim 1⅛" (2.9 cm) for patterns with a ⅝" (1.6 cm) seam allowance.

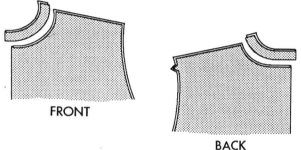

FRONT

BACK

Stitch each shoulder seam. Serge or doublestitch.

APPLYING THE COLLAR

Apply the crew neck ribbing to the neck following the procedures on pages 31–33.

Mark the center front and center back with a pin.

Divide the knit collar in half and mark with a pin.

Pin the collar to the neckline, matching the center backs and placing the ends of the collar at the center front. Pin the ends of the collar in place. The ribbing will be sandwiched between the collar and the garment.

With the collar on top, stitch over the previous stitching, stretching the collar to fit.

Press the seam allowances toward the garment.

NOTE:

The neck rib will roll slightly at the center front when the collar is in finished position.

❖❖❖❖❖

*I*f Coca Cola taught the world to sing, Stretch & Sew *taught the world to sew on knits. As I travel the country presenting sewing seminars, I discover there is a fellowship, almost a bond, among women who have taken* Stretch & Sew *classes, especially the early ones. They remember fondly such common phrases today as "sew with a relaxed bottom" and "stitch in the ditch."* Stretch & Sew *isn't just a way of sewing ... it's an attitude. At our store, we try to create a friendly, warm environment, one that feels comfortable.*

RUTHANN SPIEGELHOFF
SPIEGELHOFF'S STRETCH AND SEW
RACINE, WI

❖❖❖

Turtlenecks

A turtleneck should be made only from knit fabric to allow the high neck to pull over the head.

Basic Turtleneck

When you apply a turtleneck, you *do not* trim the neckline of the garment as you would for a crew neckband. This is because a turtleneck should start at your natural neckline and come up around your neck. Cotton interlock is especially nice for sewing turtlenecks.

Constructing the Garment

Prepare your pattern, cut your fabric, and sew the shoulder seams the same as for a Crew Neck or Mock Turtleneck (see pages 29–33). Do not trim the neckline.

NOTE:

If the pattern has ⅝″ (1.6 cm) seam allowances at the neck, trim off ⅜″ (1.0 cm). This leaves you with a ¼″ (0.6 cm) seam allowance with which to sew on the Turtleneck.

Cutting the Turtleneck

You will be applying the turtleneck with a 1:1 ratio—1″ (2.5 cm) of ribbing or knit-fabric trim to 1″ (2.5 cm) of neck edge. To determine the length for the ribbing strip, measure along the ¼″ (0.6 cm) seamline at the neck edge of the garment and add ½″ (1.3 cm) for seam allowances. Cut a strip of trim this length by 12″ (30.5 cm) wide. The greater stretch of the trim should run the length of the strip.

Applying the Turtleneck

To sew the trim to the neck, follow these steps.

Using a ¼″ *(0.6 cm) seam allowance,* sew the ends of the trim together, forming a circle. Finger-press the seam open.

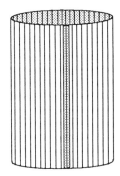

Fold the trim in half lengthwise with wrong sides together. Divide the trim into fourths and mark with pins.

Divide the neck edge of the garment into fourths and mark with pins. With the garment wrong side out, pin the trim to the neck edge, matching the seam in the trim to the center back, quarter divisions, and cut edges.

Using a *¼″ (0.6 cm) seam allowance*, stitch with the trim on top, stretching all layers as you sew.

Cowl Turtleneck

This soft, loose-fitting turtleneck does not hug the neck. A drapable fabric, such as soft sweatering, jersey, or interlock, works beautifully for this neckline.

ADAPTING THE NECK FOR A COWL COLLAR

Trim the Front pattern piece ¾″ (1.9 cm) at the center front, tapering to the shoulder edge as illustrated.

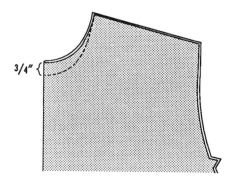

NOTE:

If the pattern has ⅝″ (1.6 cm) seam allowances at the neck, trim off ⅜″ (1.0 cm) more. This leaves you with a ¼″ (0.6 cm) seam allowance with which to sew on the cowl turtleneck.

CUTTING AND APPLYING THE COWL

Cut the cowl piece the measurement of the neck opening along the ¼″ (0.6 cm) seamline by 12″ (30.5 cm) wide for a short cowl or 16″ (40.6 cm) wide for a tall cowl.

Stitch each shoulder seam. To apply the rib cowl, refer to the procedures for the Turtleneck, pages 35–36.

❖

Turned-Under Necklines

This simple neckline is fast and easy to sew. Choose a knit that has excellent recovery to prevent the neckline from "growing."

Topstitched Neck Edge

ADAPTING THE NECK

Fold the Front and Back in half, wrong sides together.

Trim the neck ¾" (1.9 cm) for patterns with ¼" (0.6 cm) seam allowance. Trim 1⅛" (2.9 cm) away for patterns with a ⅝" (1.6 cm) seam allowance.

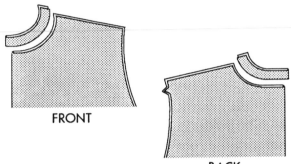

FRONT

BACK

CONSTRUCTING THE NECKLINE

Stitch the Front and Back together at the shoulder seams.

At the neck edge, fold approximately ½" (1.3 cm) to the wrong side and stitch approximately ⅜" (1.0 cm) from the folded edge. If you stretch the neck edge it may ripple. It does need some give, however, to pull over the head, so holding the fabric flat and smooth, along with the pressure of the presser foot as it feeds through the machine, will get you the ease you need.

If the neckline has stretched out, generously steam the neck area. With your fingertips, carefully push the neckline back into shape as you steam.

Shell-Stitched Neckline

The shell stitch is a pretty finish to use on a turned-under neckline. This is done using an overcast or shell stitch on your machine.

Sew the neckline following the procedure for the Topstitched Neck Edge (see page 37).

Set the machine for an overcast or shell stitch.

NOTE:

Test the stitch on a scrap of fabric before sewing on garment.

Stitch on the right side of the garment ¼" (0.6 cm) from the fold so that the zigzag stitch goes slightly over the fold.

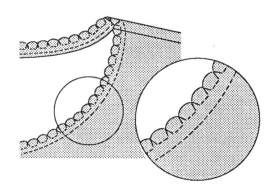

If the neckline has stretched out, generously steam the neck area and, with your fingertips, carefully push the neckline back into shape as you steam.

Neckline With French Trim

For this neckline, fabric is used for the French Trim finish. The French Trim strip can be cut from any knit fabric with at least 25-percent stretch. The stretch is needed to allow the trim to go around the curve of the neckline and still lie flat.

Constructing the Neckline

You will need a pattern with a scooped neckline that is wide enough to pull over your head without using an opening for a zipper or back slit.

ADAPTING THE NECK ON AN EXISTING PATTERN

You can adjust a high neck pattern by trimming the neckline. Keep in mind that the trim will finish at the cut edge of the neck.

First trim away any seam allowance at the neckline. If, when Front and Back are pinned together, the neck doesn't pull over your head easily, then scoop mostly on the front so the shoulders don't become too wide. Be sure the Front and Back shoulder widths end up the same. To start, try trimming approximately 1" (2.5 cm) from the center front, tapering to ¼" (0.6 cm) at the shoulders. Trim ¼" (0.6 cm) from back neck. Then baste the shoulders and try on the garment to be sure it will pull over head.

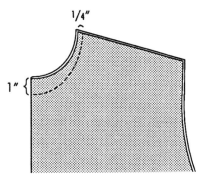

Constructing the Trim

CUTTING THE TRIM STRIPS

French Trim can be made in varying widths. The width of the cut strip should be four times the width of the finished trim.

To determine the correct trim-strip width and seam allowance, refer to the Trim Strip Measurement Chart (next page).

❖

Trim Strip Measurement Chart

For This Finished Width	Cut Strip This Wide*	Stitch with This Seam Allowance
¼″ (0.6 cm)	1″ (2.5 cm)	¼″ (0.6 cm)
⅜″ (1.0 cm)	1½″ (3.8 cm)	⅜″ (1.0 cm)
½″ (1.3 cm)	2″ (5.1 cm)	½″ (1.3 cm)
⅝″ (1.6 cm)	2½″ (6.4 cm)	⅝″ (1.6 cm)

* For bulkier knit fabric such as a textured sweater knit, add another ¼″ (0.6 cm) to the width. The bulk of the fabric takes up the extra width when it is turned.

Cut the trim strip the length of the neck opening plus 12″ (30.5 cm) by the determined width, with the greater stretch of the fabric going the length of the strip.

Applying the Trim

Stitch each shoulder seam.

Fold the garment in half to find the center back. Measure 3″ (7.6 cm) from each side of the center back and mark the neckline with pins. The two 3″ (7.6 cm) sections across the back of the neck will remain unsewn to allow room for completing the trim-strip splice at the center back.

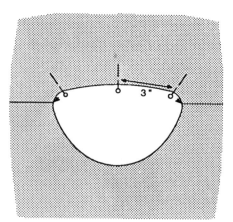

Since the amount of trim necessary to make a bias splice is equal to the opened width of the trim, you need to leave a tail at least *half* that amount plus the 3″ (7.6 cm) at center back. I prefer to leave 5″ (12.7 cm) of trim so that I have plenty to work with. Place a pin 5″ (12.7 cm) from one end of the trim strip. With right sides together, match this point to one of the side pins on the neck edge as illustrated.

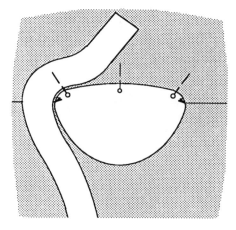

Matching the cut edges, pin the strip to the Front neckline between the pins. Stitch with the *determined seam allowance* (see chart on page 40) from pin to pin, stretching slightly around curves.

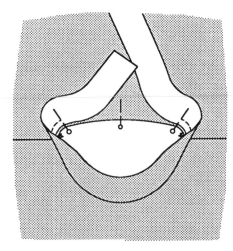

Cut a 3″ (7.6 cm) piece off the end of the longest strip. Fold in half and press along the 3″ (7.6 cm) length. You will use this as a guide for trimming your strips to the correct length. Matching the cut edges, lay the *left* strip along the back neck edge. Place the strip guide along the neck edge, centering the crease of the guide over the center back marking.

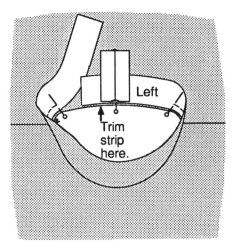

Trim the strip as indicated.

Unpin the guide strip. Repeat for the *right* side.

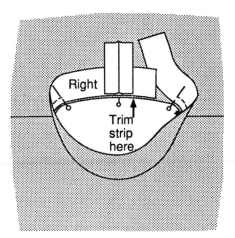

Trim the strip where indicated.

To splice, place the ends of the strip *right sides* together at a 90-degree angle and pin. Mark a line along the seamline from corner to corner as illustrated.

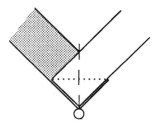

Baste first. Then check to see that when the splice is sewn the cut edges will be even. If they are correct, go ahead and stitch.

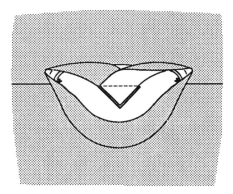

❖

Trim the splice seam allowances to ¼" (0.6 cm) from your stitching. Press the seam open.

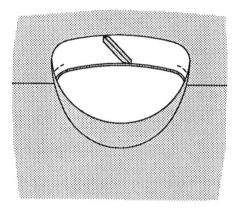

Complete the stitching along the back neckline. Then carefully press the trim and seam allowances away from the garment.

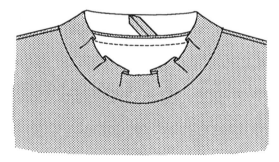

Fold the trim strip over the seam allowances to the wrong side of the garment. The fold of the trim should be right against the cut edges of the seam allowances. Pin the trim in place.

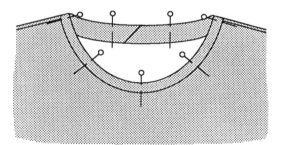

NOTE:

Since knits do not ravel, it is not necessary to finish the inside edge of the trim. If you do want a nice stitched finish, follow these simple instructions. After you have pinned the trim in place, mark a line on the inside edge of the trim ¼" (0.6 cm) below the trim seamline. (You'll need to unpin a section to see the seamline.)

Remove the pins and cut off the excess trim below the line you marked. Serge or zigzag along the cut edge of the trim. Repin the trim in position.

Secure with one of the following methods:

• Stitch-in-the-ditch by sewing into the seamline from the right side of the garment.

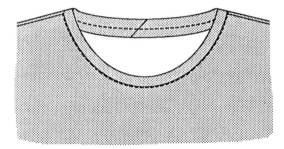

• From the right side, edgestitch on the strip next to the seamline.

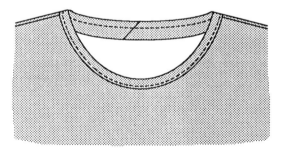

❖

- Using a double needle, straddle the seam and topstitch the strip from the right side.

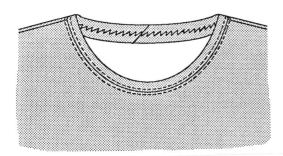

Trim the strip close to the stitching.

V-Necklines

V-necklines can be finished with ribbing, rib bands, or knit self-fabric. A V-neck gives a larger opening so the garment will pull over the head without a zipper or back opening.

Adapting Your Pattern for a V-Neckline

If your pattern does not have a V-neckline, you can draw your own using a pattern with a natural neckline.

If your pattern has ⅝″ (1.6 cm) seam allowances, trim ⅜″ (1.0 cm) from the Front and Back neck edges only, giving your pattern a ¼″ (0.6 cm) seam allowance at the neck edge.

Measure approximately 5″ (12.7 cm) from the neck edge along the center front and mark. Draw a line to the shoulder edge.

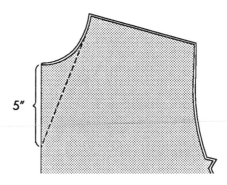

Trim along the drawn line. Use this pattern and choose the V-neck finish you prefer. Some techniques will call for additional trimming to allow for the trim to be sewn on.

Mitered V-Neck

A mitered V-neck is a pretty finish for a neckline and easy to sew.

❖

Adapting the Neck

If your pattern does not have a V-neckline, see page 43 for creating your own.

Trim the Front and Back V-necklines 1″ (2.5 cm) to allow for the trim to be sewn on.

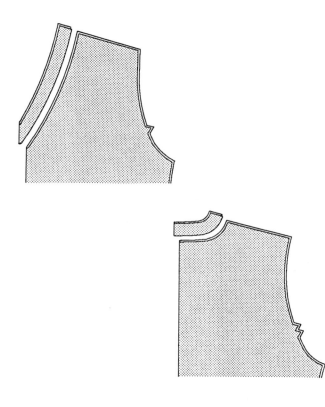

Cutting the Trim Strips

From ribbing or knit fabric, cut the Trim Strip 3″ (7.6 cm) wide by the measurement of the neck edge along the ¼″ (0.6 cm) seamline plus ½″ (1.3 cm). Cut with greater stretch going the length of the strip.

Constructing the Garment

Stitch each shoulder seam. Serge or doublestitch. Reinforce the point of the V by stitching on the ¼″ (0.6 cm) seamline 1″ (2.5 cm) on each side of the point, using a shorter stitch length.

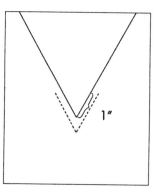

Clip to the point of the V, being careful not to clip through stitching.

Applying the Trim

With wrong sides together, fold the trim in half lengthwise. Measure the garment from the center back to the shoulder seam along the ¼″ (0.6 cm) seamline. Take ⅔ of that measurement and add ¼″ (0.6 cm). Place a pin that distance from one cut end of the trim.

❖

Matching the pin in the trim to the right shoulder seam, pin the trim along the neck edge to the point of the V.

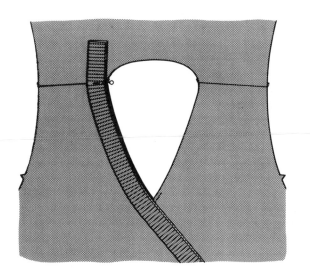

Open the trim and, with right sides together, stitch across the ends. Finger-press the seam open.

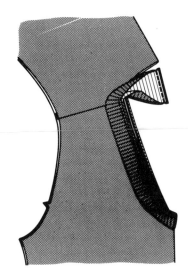

With the trim on top and the fabric next to the machine, stitch from the pin to the point of the V, stretching the trim *slightly*. Leaving the needle in the fabric, lift the presser foot and pull the unstitched side of the neckline down to straighten the point of the V. Continue stitching to the left shoulder seam.

Remove the garment from the machine. Cut a strip of trim on the left back neck to the same length as on the right back neck.

Refold the ribbing with wrong sides together.

Matching the seam in the trim to the center back, stitch the trim to the back neckline, stretching the trim to fit.

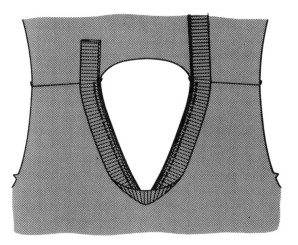

❖

To miter the point of the V, fold the garment in half at the center front with right sides together, making sure the edges of the trim are even. Clip the rib seam allowance at the point of the V, being careful not to cut through the stitching. Backstitch to the folded edges of the rib and sew exactly to the point of the V. Backstitch again.

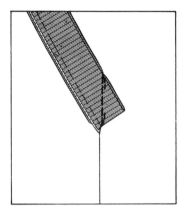

Clip the ribbing to the point of the V, being careful not to cut through the stitching. Finger-press the seam open. To secure the cut ends of the trim, stitch over the previous stitching through the seam allowances. (Do not catch the Front in the stitching.)

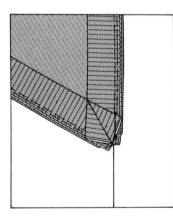

Narrow Crossover V-Neck

An easy technique for a classic V.

❖

ADAPTING THE NECK

If your pattern does not have a V-neckline, see page 43 for creating your own.

Trim the Front and Back necklines 1″ (2.5 cm) to allow for the trim to be sewn on.

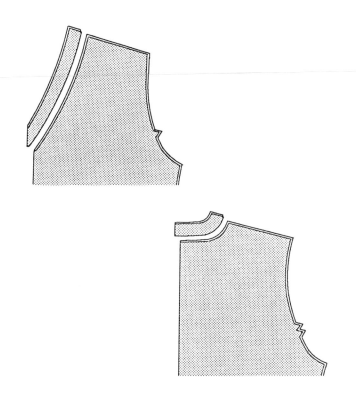

CUTTING THE TRIM STRIPS

From the ribbing or knit fabric, cut the Trim Strip 3″ (7.6 cm) wide by the measurement of the neck edge along the ¼″ (0.6 cm) seamline plus 5″ (12.7 cm). Cut so that the greater stretch runs along the length of the strip.

CONSTRUCTING THE GARMENT

Stitch each shoulder seam. Serge or doublestitch.

Reinforce the point of the V by stitching on the ¼″ (0.6 cm) seamline 1″ (2.5 cm) on each side of the point, using a shorter stitch length.

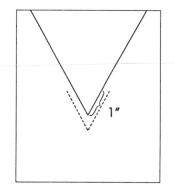

APPLYING THE TRIM

Place a pin at the point of the V on the seamline so that when stitching the trim to the garment you can see it easily.

Fold the strip in half lengthwise with wrong sides together. On the left side of the neckline, match the cut edges of the trim to the V-neckline, leaving approximately 3″ (7.6 cm) extending below the point of the V. Using a ¼″ (0.6 cm) seam allowance, *backstitch* exactly to the point of the V, removing the pin as necessary, then stitch to the shoulder seam, stretching the trim slightly.

Measure the distance across the back neck. Determine a 2:3 ratio. Measure this distance on the trim from the left shoulder seam and mark with a pin. Match the pin to the right shoulder seam. Stitch the trim across the back neck, stretching the trim slightly to fit the garment.

Stretching the trim slightly, continue stitching the remainder of the trim to the right side of the neckline, stopping 2″ (5.2 cm) from the point of the V.

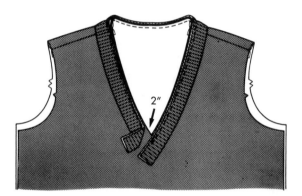

Clip the garment only to the stitching at the point of the V.

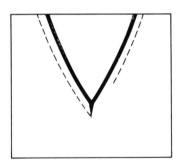

Turn the trim to the finished position, tucking the extensions to the wrong side of the garment, lapping left over right. Pin the trim in position through all layers, making sure the neckline and trim lie flat.

Fold the garment Front to expose the ends of the trim. Backstitch to the point of the V, then sew to the previous stitching.

Stitch over the previous stitching to fasten the remaining end of the trim. Trim the ends of the trim.

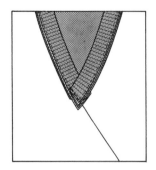

❖

Wide Crossover V-Neck

This V-neck crosses over like the previous garment, but because you will use a wider width of rib, it finishes higher on the neck.

ADAPTING THE NECK

If your pattern does not have a V-neckline, see page 43 for creating your own.

CUTTING THE TRIM

Cut a strip of ribbing 7″ (17.8 cm) wide by the measurement of the neck edge along the ¼″ (0.6 cm) seamline plus 5″ (12.7 cm).

CONSTRUCTING THE GARMENT

Stitch each shoulder seam. Reinforce the point of the V by stitching on the ¼″ (0.6 cm) seamline 1″ (2.5 cm) on each side of the point, using a shorter stitch length.

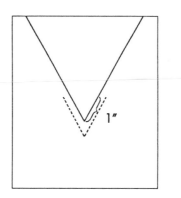

Place a pin at the point of the V on the seamline so that you can see it easily when stitching the trim to the garment.

APPLYING THE TRIM

Fold the strip in half lengthwise with wrong sides together. On the left side of the neckline, match the cut edges of the ribbing to the V-neckline, leaving approximately 3″ (7.6 cm) extending below the point of the V. Using a ¼″ (0.6 cm) seam allowance, *backstitch* exactly to the point of the V, removing the pin as necessary, then stitch to the shoulder seam, stretching the ribbing slightly.

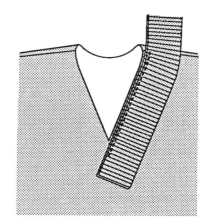

❖

Measure the distance across the back neck. Determine a 2:3 ratio. Measure this distance on the rib from the left shoulder seam and mark with a pin. Match the pin to the right shoulder seam. Stitch the ribbing to the back neckline, stretching the ribbing to fit. Stretching the rib slightly, continue stitching the remainder of the ribbing to the right side of the neckline, stopping 4″ (10.2 cm) from the point of the V.

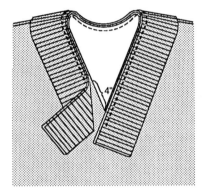

Clip the garment only to the stitching at the point of the V.

Turn the ribbing to the finished position, tucking the extensions to the wrong side of the garment, lapping left over right. Pin the ribbing in position through all layers, making sure the neckline and ribbing lie flat.

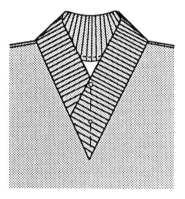

Fold the garment Front to expose the ends of ribbing. Backstitch to the point of the V, then sew to the previous stitching.

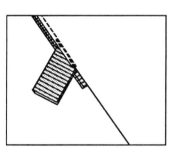

Stitch over the previous stitching to fasten the remaining end of the ribbing. Trim the ends of the ribbing.

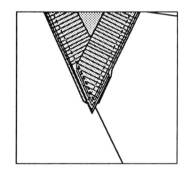

Rugby Necklines

A rugby neckline is a versatile neck opening because it can be made any length desired.

Basic Construction

Start with a pattern with a rugby opening. If your pattern doesn't have a rugby opening, trace the one provided on page 124. The notched side is angled, but it will be straight when the garment is finished.

OPENING OPTIONS

You can change the opening to the length you prefer by lengthening or shortening the stitching lines, keeping them ¼" (0.6 cm) apart at the top and ⅛" (0.3 cm) apart at the point. Facing piece should extend 1" (2.5 cm) beyond the point of the stitching lines at the lower edge.

Classic opening—
6 " (15.2 cm)

Long opening—
12 " (30.5 cm)

❖

CUTTING THE RUGBY FACING

The Rugby Facing and Neck Facing Strip work best if cut from a lightweight fabric that is not bulky. I like to use a woven broadcloth because of the great range of colors this fabric comes in. The tight weave helps secure the point of the slash and keeps it from pulling out.

From the *fabric*, cut one Rugby Facing *with the right side of the fabric up.*

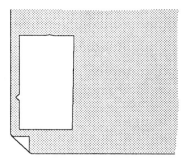

From the *fusible knit or woven interfacing*, cut one Facing *with the adhesive side up.*

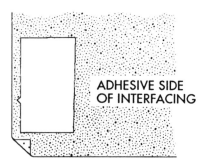

ADHESIVE SIDE
OF INTERFACING

Transfer all construction marks to the right side of the interfacing. Fuse the interfacing to the Rugby Facing.

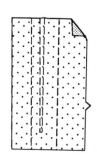

APPLYING THE RUGBY

Mark the center front on the Front garment piece.

With *right* sides together, pin the Facing to the Front, matching the neck edges and the center front placement line on the Facing to the center front marking on the front of the garment.

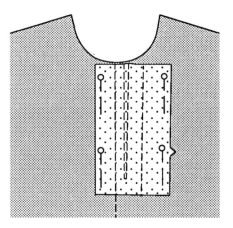

Using a shorter stitch length, sew along the stitching lines for the slash through all thicknesses. Sew one stitch across the point of the slash to make turning easier.

❖

Cut down the center of the slash through all thicknesses, being careful not to cut through the stitching.

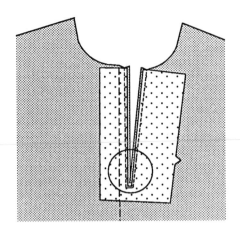

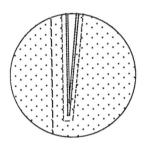

Turn the Facing to the *wrong* side of the garment. Press the right side of the slash carefully, rolling the seam slightly to the underside. Along each side edge of the Facing, press under ½″ (1.3 cm).

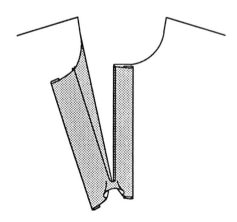

Edgestitch along the pressed edge of the right tab only.

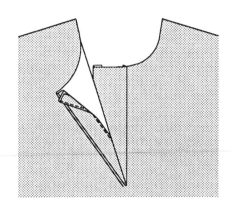

On the left Facing, press the seam allowances toward the Facing. Form a 1″-wide (2.5 cm) tab by folding the Facing, wrong sides together, on the foldline and matching the center fronts. Press carefully.

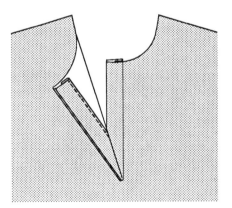

CONSTRUCTING THE GARMENT

Stitch each shoulder seam. Now you are ready to add the collar or neckline finish of your choice.

❖

Rugby with Collar

COLLAR OPTIONS

You can choose from the many purchased knit collars available or create a collar from the same knit you used to sew the shirt (in which case the collar is called a *self-fabric collar*). Coordinating fabric can also be used.

Choosing a Purchased Collar

A purchased knit collar has three finished edges; the edge you sew to the neck is unfinished. The collar should be at least 3″ (7.6 cm) wide by 15″ (38.1 cm) long.

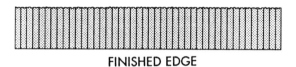

FINISHED EDGE

Creating a Self-Fabric Collar

Draw a pattern for a square collar.

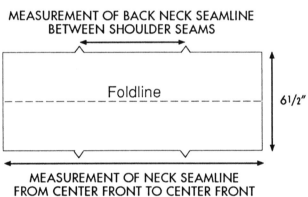

MEASUREMENT OF BACK NECK SEAMLINE
BETWEEN SHOULDER SEAMS

Foldline

6¹/₂″

MEASUREMENT OF NECK SEAMLINE
FROM CENTER FRONT TO CENTER FRONT
PLUS SEAM ALLOWANCE AT EACH END

Interface half of the Collar. Fold the Collar right sides together along the foldline. Stitch each end.

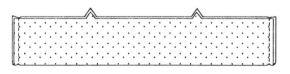

Turn the Collar right side out and press, rolling the seams slightly to the noninterfaced side. Edgestitch the finished edges.

❖

APPLYING THE COLLAR

Pin the purchased knit collar or noninterfaced side of the self-fabric Collar to the right side of the garment, matching the cut edges, the notches on the Collar to the shoulder seams, and the ends of the Collar to the center fronts.

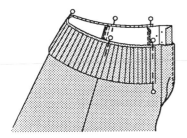

PURCHASED COLLAR

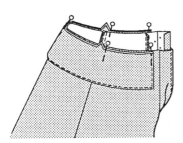

FABRIC COLLAR

Then stitch.

Fold the Facing extensions, right sides together, over the Collar, matching the center front markings and the cut edges at the neckline. Stitch in place.

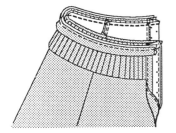

CUTTING THE NECK FACING STRIP

Cut the *Neck Facing Strip* from the same fabric as the Rugby Facing (with the greater stretch going the length of the strip for knits; cut on the bias for wovens) 1⅜″ (3.5 cm) wide by 19″ (48.3 cm) long.

Press the Neck Facing Strip in half lengthwise with wrong sides together.

APPLYING THE NECK FACING STRIP

Matching the cut edges, pin the Strip to the Collar with a 1:1 ratio. Trim the ends of the Strip even with the center front. Stitch over the previous stitching.

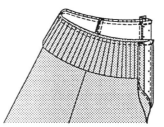

Trim the corners and seam allowances close to the stitching. Turn the Facing extensions to the finished position and press. Press the Strip and seam allowances toward the garment. From the inside, edgestitch the Strip to the garment, beginning and ending the stitching just over the right and left edges of the Facing.

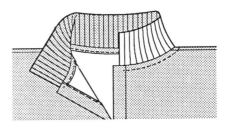

Edgestitch the left side of the Facing next to the Facing seamline, or stitch-in-the-ditch, catching the pressed edge on the underside.

FINISHING THE COLLAR WITHOUT NECK FACING STRIP

If you are not using a Neck Facing Strip, zigzag or serge over the seam allowances of the collar and follow the directions below. Turn the Facing extensions to the finished position and press. Press the neckline seam allowances toward the garment.

Topstitch on the garment, catching the seam allowance on the underside and beginning and ending the stitching just over the right and left edges of the Facing.

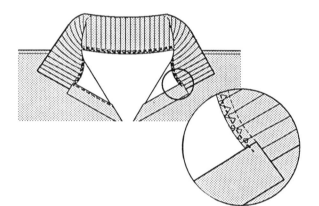

Edgestitch the left side of the Facing next to the Facing seamline, catching the pressed edge on the underside, or stitch-in-the-ditch.

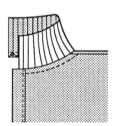

COMPLETING THE RUGBY APPLICATION

Place the Front in the finished position and press. Stitch through all thicknesses on the lower edge of the opening as illustrated.

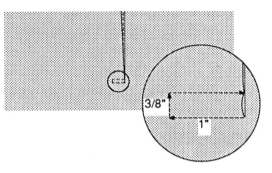

Lift the Front and trim the Facing end to ½″ (1.3 cm) from the stitching. Zigzag or serge over the cut edges.

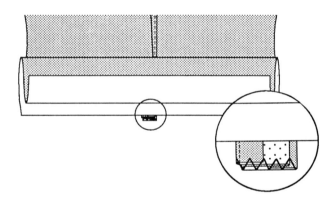

Machine stitch ⅝″ (1.6 cm) vertical buttonholes along the center front on the right Front. Begin the top buttonhole ½″ (1.3 cm) below the neck seamline. Equally space two more buttonholes for the classic length; and four more buttonholes for the long length. Sew the buttons in place on the left Front.

❖

Rugby with French Trim

French Trim is a versatile finish and so easy to do.

ADAPTING THE NECK

Trim away any neckline seam allowances.

CONSTRUCTING THE RUGBY

Apply the rugby according to the instructions on pages 51–56, disregarding all references to the Collar applications and neckline stitching.

CUTTING THE TRIM

The trim strip can be cut from any knit fabric that has at least 25-percent stretch. The stretch is necessary to allow the trim to go around the curve of the neckline and still lie flat.

Cut the trim strip according to the determined measurement in the chart below by the neckline measurement along the ¼″ (0.6 cm) seamline plus 2″ (5.1 cm).

APPLYING THE TRIM

Leaving ½″ (1.3 cm) extending at one side of the front neck opening, stitch the trim strip to the garment, stretching slightly, with the rugby facings in the finished position as illustrated.

TRIM STRIP MEASUREMENT CHART

For This Finished Width	Cut Strip This Wide*	Stitch with This Seam Allowance
½ ″ (1.3 cm)	2¼″ (5.7 cm)	½″ (1.3 cm)
⅜″ (1.0 cm)	1¾″ (4.4 cm)	⅜″ (1.0 cm)
¼″ (0.6 cm)	1¼″ (5.1 cm)	¼″ (1.6 cm)

* For bulkier knit fabric such as a textured sweater knit, add another ¼″ (0.6 cm) to the width.
  The bulk of the fabric takes up the extra width when it is turned.

❖

Trim the excess from the trim strip to ½" (1.3 cm) at the other side of the opening.

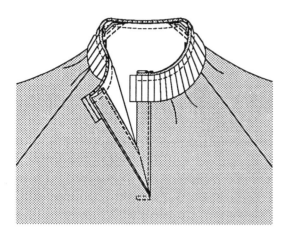

Press the trim strip and seam allowances toward the neck opening.

Fold the strip, right sides together, as illustrated and pin in position. Stitch across each end of the strip so that the strip is even with the folded edge of the garment. Do not doublestitch.

Turn the ends right side out.

Fold the strip toward the center so that the cut edges meet. Then fold the strip again to the wrong side, enclosing the cut edges.

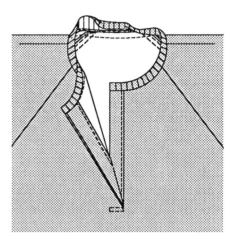

Edgestitch on the trim, being sure to catch the fold on the underside.

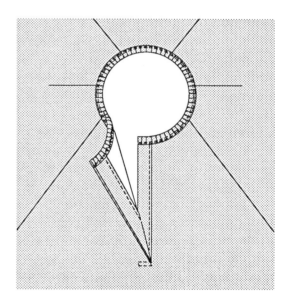

Machine stitch ⅝" (1.6 cm) vertical buttonholes along the center front on the right Front. Begin the top buttonhole ¼" (0.6 cm) below the neck seamline. Equally space two more buttonholes for the classic length; and four more buttonholes for the long length. Sew the buttons in place on the left Front.

3 CARDIGANS

Cardigans are among the most classic and versatile of all garments. They coordinate well with pants, skirts, and dresses in both formal and casual looks. And best of all, they are wonderfully practical while keeping you warm and fashionable at the same time.

All fabric weights work well for cardigans. Doubleknit, sweatshirting, jersey, and interlock are all great choices.

The front of your cardigan can be finished with ribbing. The lower edge can be finished with ribbing or hemmed. Make the cardigans any length you want. Check your pattern for the length you prefer. Add a patch pocket with rib trim at the top to complete the look.

Regardless of your choice of finish for your cardigan, the basic construction is the same.

❖

Cardigan with Ribbed Trim

Constructing the Cardigan

ADAPTING THE NECK

If your cardigan front does not have a V-neck, you will need to give it one for this technique. If your pattern has ⅝″ (1.6 cm) seam allowances, trim ⅜″ (1.0 cm) from the Front and Back necklines to provide a ¼″ (0.6 cm) seam allowance at the neckline.

On the Front, draw a line along the center front. Mark a point approximately 2″ (5.1 cm) above the waist at the center front. Mark another point on the shoulder ½″ (1.3 cm) away from the neck edge. Draw a line from the shoulder point to the center front point. Fold away the excess pattern along the front edge and neckline.

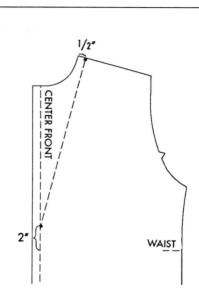

On the Back, trim ½″ (1.3 cm) from the neck edge.

ADDING PATCH POCKETS WITH RIB TRIM

If you're using a patch pocket pattern you already have, trim 1½″ (3.8 cm) off the top finished edge to allow for the added trim. If you're drawing a patch pocket pattern, determine the finished measurements you want and add a ⅝″ (1.6 cm) seam allowance at the sides and bottom and allow for the 1¼″ (3.2 cm) wide rib trim that will be added at top.

Cut two strips of ribbing 4″ (10.2 cm) wide by the width of the pocket top edge.

Fold each strip in half lengthwise, right sides together, and stitch across the ends with a ⅝″ (1.6 cm) seam allowance.

Trim the seam allowances. Turn to the finished position and press lightly.

Place the ribbing at the top of the Pocket. Fold the *⅝″ (1.6 cm)* Pocket seam allowances over the ribbing at each side edge and pin.

Stitch across the top of the Pocket *with a ¼″ (0.6 cm) seam allowance.*

Turn to the finished position. Press the seam allowances to the wrong side on the side and lower edges of the Pocket.

Pin the Pockets to the Fronts. Edgestitch in position.

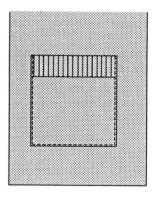

❖

CONSTRUCTING THE SLEEVES

Stitch each shoulder seam. Press the seam allowance to the back.

Pin each Sleeve to the garment and stitch.

Serge the edge or doublestitch. Press the seam allowances toward the Sleeve.

To serge side seams and rib cuffs, refer to page 28.

To sew the seams, stitch each side seam from the lower edge of the garment to the lower edge of the Sleeve, matching the underarm seams.

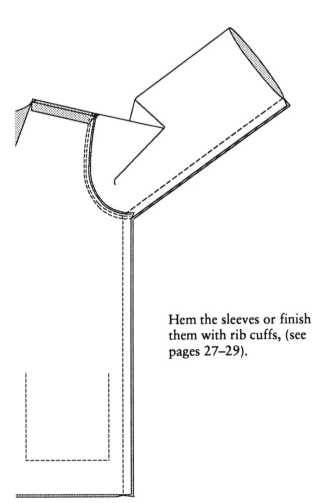

Hem the sleeves or finish them with rib cuffs, (see pages 27–29).

Creating a Ribbed Lower Edge

Coordinate the trim on your cardigan by adding ribbing to the lower edge. Instructions for omitting the ribbing and simply hemming the cardigan instead are included on page 64. These instructions allow for a 3″ (7.6 cm) finished ribbed band. Check for the desired length of your cardigan before adding the rib.

CUTTING THE RIB

For the lower rib band, cut a strip of ribbing 6½″ (16.5 cm) wide by ¾ the measurement of the lower edge of the garment.

NOTE:

On larger sizes, if piecing is necessary, cut two strips of ribbing 6 ½″ (16.5 cm) wide by ¾ the measurement of one Front lower edge plus ¼″ (0.6 cm) for the seam allowance. Cut one strip of ribbing ¾ the measurement of the Back lower edge plus ½″ (1.3 cm) for the seam allowances. Stitch the strips together with a ½″ (0.6 cm) seam allowance.

APPLYING THE RIB

With wrong sides together, fold the ribbing in half lengthwise, matching the cut edges. Divide the ribbing and the garment lower edge into fourths and mark the quarter divisions with pins.

Pin the ribbing to the garment, matching the quarter divisions and the cut edges. Using a ¼″ (0.6 cm) seam allowance, stitch with the ribbing on top, stretching ribbing to fit.

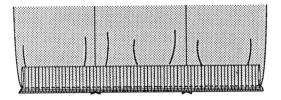

Serge or doublestitch. Turn the ribbing to the finished position.

❖

Finishing the Cardigan

CUTTING THE TRIM

To finish the front edge, cut two strips of trim 4″ (10.2 cm) wide by the measurement of the garment from the lower edge to the center back plus 4″ (10.2 cm). Piece if necessary.

Fold each strip of trim in half lengthwise, right sides together. Stitch across one end, using a ¼″ (0.6 cm) seam allowance.

Turn right side out and lightly press the strip in half lengthwise, being careful not to stretch the strip.

APPLYING THE TRIM

With right sides together and matching the cut edges, place the ribbing strip on the *left* Front of the garment with the stitched end even with the folded edge of the lower ribbing. Pin the strip to the garment from the lower edge to the left shoulder seam, making sure the ribbing lies flat and does not pull the garment.

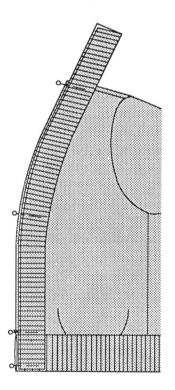

Since different types of ribbing vary greatly in weight and stretch memory, each one needs to be handled a little differently in order for it to lie smooth and flat on the garment. Too much rib along the front opening will make the hem droop; too little will pull the hem up. The best way to find the correct proportion is to pin the strip of ribbing to the lower edge of your garment and, while holding the garment at the pin, stretch the strip of ribbing. Then let the ribbing relax and pin it along the front opening in this position.

Stitch the ribbing to the garment from the lower edge to the left shoulder seam.

Cut the extending piece of trim to ⅔ the measurement from the shoulder seam to the center back.

Using a cutoff piece of trim as a guide, trim the same amount from the unfinished end of the strip for the *right side*. Measure the unstitched trim on the left Front from the shoulder to the cut edge. Place a pin in the right trim this same distance to mark the shoulder point.

With right sides together and matching the cut edges, pin the trim strip to the *right* front as before, placing a pin in the rib at the shoulder seam. Stitch the ribbing to the garment from the lower edge to the right shoulder seam.

FINISHING THE BACK NECK

At the center back, open the ends of the trim and, with right sides together, stitch across the ends with a ¼″ (0.6 cm) seam allowance.

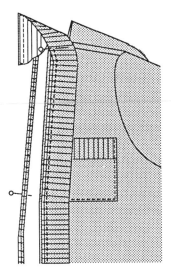

Refold the trim with wrong sides together. Pin the trim to the back neckline, matching the seam in the trim to the center back. Stitch with a ¼″ (0.6 cm) seam allowance, stretching the trim to fit across the back neck.

Serge or doublestitch. Turn the trim to the finished position and lightly press the seam allowances toward the garment.

ADDING BUTTONS AND BUTTONHOLES

Mark vertical buttonholes along the center of the ribbing on the right Front, placing the top buttonhole at the V point and the bottom buttonhole 2½″ (6.4 cm) from the lower edge of the garment.

Equally space the remaining buttonholes.

Try on the garment to be sure you have placed the buttonholes correctly.

To sew the buttonholes, see the instructions on pages 23–24.

Cardigan with Hemmed Lower Edge

Constructing the Cardigan

Follow the basic instructions for adapting the neck and constructing the sleeves given in Cardigan with Ribbed Trim (pages 60–61).

Press in the hem at the lower edge of the garment, but do not stitch in place yet.

Finishing the Cardigan

ADDING THE FRONT EDGE TRIM

Cut the strip for the front edge finish and prepare it according to the procedures on page 62, placing the stitched end of the trim strip at the fold of the hem. Fold the hem to the right side over the trim and pin it in position.

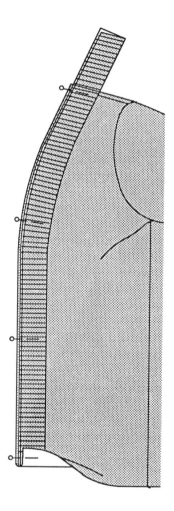

FINISHING THE BACK NECK

Stitch from the lower edge to the left shoulder. Complete the application of the trim using the procedures on page 63, placing the stitched end of the trim at the fold of the hem as before.

HEMMING THE CARDIGAN

Turn the hem to the finished position. Beginning and ending at the trim seamlines, stitch the hem in the garment.

ADDING BUTTONS AND BUTTONHOLES

To mark buttonhole placement, use the procedures on page 63.

To stitch, see the instructions on pages 23-24.

4 PANTS & SKIRTS

I n this chapter you'll learn how to make pull-on pants and skirts with great pockets. You'll discover easy elastic-waist finishes and how to make a simple crotch-depth adjustment on pants. I recommend that you use a knit that is not too stretchy when making pants or skirts. Select a fabric that will not bag at the knees or "sit out" on the backside. Doubleknits usually work best. For wider-leg pants or fuller skirts, choose an interlock or jersey.

Choosing a Pattern

Determining Your Pattern Size

Your hip measurement will determine the pattern size you choose for your pants or skirt. Take your hip measurement 9″ (23.0 cm) below the waist or at the fullest part of your hip, measuring over the undergarments you will wear with the pants.

To be sure you are measuring from your natural waistline, tie a string around your middle. The string will settle at your natural waist, the narrowest part of your middle.

To take your hip measurement, hold the tape so that it's snug against your hips but not tight. You should be able to feel the tape against your body, yet it should be loose enough to slide back and forth.

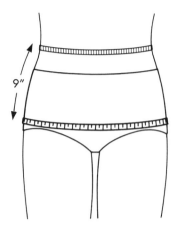

Now take your waist measurement, holding the tape so that it's snug against your waist but not tight.

Adjusting Your Pattern for Better Fit

ADJUSTING THE CROTCH DEPTH

Many ready-to-wear pants appear to be the wrong size because they are too long or too short in the crotch.

To determine correct crotch depth, take a sit measurement. Tie a string around your waist. Sit on a hard surface with your feet flat on the floor. Measure from the string at your natural waistline, over the curve of your hip, and straight down to the flat surface. Sit up straight—you will get an incorrect measurement if you lean over to look at the tape.

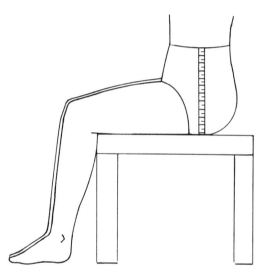

Compare your sit measurement with the crotch depth given for your size on the chart below:

STRETCH & SEW PANTS PATTERN CROTCH DEPTH (SIT MEASUREMENT)

Size	Inches	Centimeters
32	9¼	23.5
34	9½	24.1
36	9¾	24.8
38	10	25.4
40	10¼	26.0
42	10½	26.7
44	10¾	27.3
46	11	27.9
48	11¼	28.6

If the measurements are not the same, you must make an adjustment on the Front and Back pattern pieces. Cut at the shorten or lengthen line for the crotch depth and add or subtract the difference between the measurements.

Example of Lengthening the Crotch Depth

If the sit measurement corresponding to your size is 10″ (25.4 cm) and your own sit measurement is 10½″ (26.7 cm), *add ½″* (1.3 cm) to the Front and Back pattern pieces.

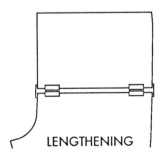

LENGTHENING

Example of Shortening the Crotch Depth

If the sit measurement corresponding to your size is 10″ (25.4 cm) and your own sit measurement is 9½″ (24.1 cm), *subtract ½″* (1.3 cm) from the Front and Back pattern pieces.

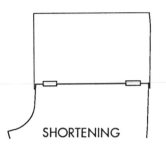

SHORTENING

ADJUSTING THE WAIST

Compare your waist measurement to the waist measurement on the pattern for your size. If your waist measurement is larger than the one given for your size, cut or trace your pattern in a larger size at the waist.

If your waist measurement is smaller than the one given on the pattern for your size, cut or trace the pattern smaller at the waist. Because you are making pull-on pants, remember that they must pull up over the hips. Don't make too big an adjustment. Rely on the elastic to draw in the waistline of your pants.

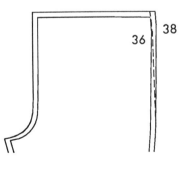

36   38

Adjusting the Pants Length

The best way to determine pants length is to put on a pair of pants that fits you well and also to put on the shoes you plan to wear with the finished pants. Measure at the side seam from your waist to your hemline. Compare this measurement to your pants pattern, measuring from the waistline to the hemline along the side seam.

If necessary, shorten or lengthen the pattern pieces at the lower edge or at the shorten/lengthen lines on the legs as you cut out or trace your pattern.

❖❖❖❖❖

*A*nn Person taught us to share everything freely and not to hold back anything. As a result, our customers also shared ideas freely, so we learned equally from them.

JUDY LAUBE
LAUBE'S *STRETCH & SEW*
BLOOMINGTON, MN

❖❖❖

Adding Pockets: Four Options

If the pattern you are using does not already have a pocket, be sure there is enough ease in the hip area to accommodate one. If there are pleats or gathers at the waist edge, there is probably plenty of room.

The pockets and dimensions in this section are for pants using a turned-down 1¼" (3.2 cm) elastic waist. If you are using a different waist treatment, adjust the pockets accordingly.

One-Piece Slash Pockets

A slash pocket is a classic look you can add to many pants. Follow these steps to construct an easy one-piece slash pocket. Remember to start with a pattern that has a turned-down 1¼" (3.2 cm) elastic waist.

❖

CUTTING THE POCKETS

To draw a pocket, follow the grid illustration.

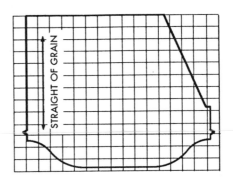

1 square = 1 inch (2.5 cm)

When the pocket is folded in half, the side edges of the Pocket and the Front pattern piece should match when the upper edges are lined up. Trim Pocket pattern piece if necessary.

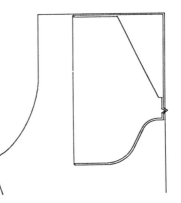

Cut two pockets from the fabric.

From fusible interfacing, cut two strips 1″ (2.5 cm) wide by the length of the angled edge of the Pocket pattern piece.

Bond one strip to the wrong side of each Pocket.

❖

SEWING THE POCKETS

Pin a Pocket to each Front, matching the upper and side edges.

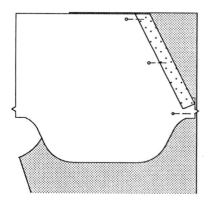

Trim the Front even with the Pocket.

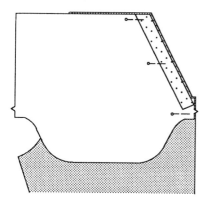

With right sides together, pin each Pocket to each Front, matching cut edges. Stitch with a ¼″ (0.6 cm) seam allowance, pivoting at the dot and stitching to the side edge.

Clip to dot, being careful not to clip through the stitching.

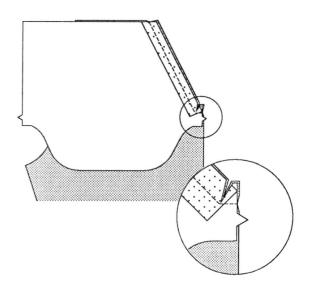

Press the seam open where possible, for ease in turning. Press the Pocket to the wrong side of the garment, rolling the seam slightly to the underside.

Edgestitch the Pocket opening, pivoting at the corner.

Topstitch ¼″ (0.6 cm) from the previous stitching.

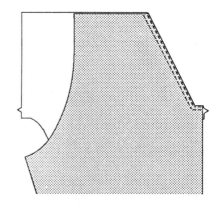

❖

With right sides together, press the Pocket in half, matching the cut edges and the notches.

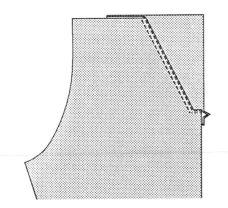

Pin the Pocket in the finished position.

Edgestitch and topstitch through all layers on the upper 2½″ (6.4 cm) of the Pocket opening, sewing over the previous stitching.

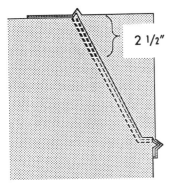

2 1/2″

Stitch the lower edges of the Pocket together.

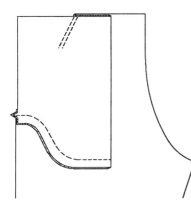

Machine baste the Pocket in place just inside the seamline on the side edge.

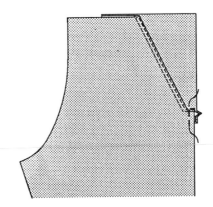

Machine baste the Pocket 1¾″ (4.4 cm) from the waist edge and trim both layers of the Pocket as illustrated.

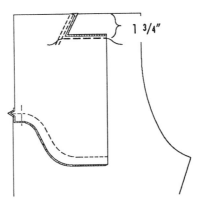

1 3/4″

Curved Pockets

For a softer look, use a pocket with a curved opening. Remember to start with a pattern that has a turned-down 1¼″ (3.2 cm) elastic waist.

CUTTING THE POCKETS

To draw a pocket, use the grid illustration.

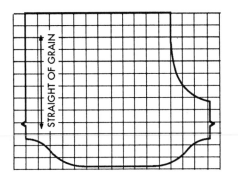

1 square = 1 inch (2.5 cm)

When the Pocket is folded in half, the side edges of the Pocket and the Front pattern piece should match when the upper edges are lined up. Trim Pocket pattern piece if necessary.

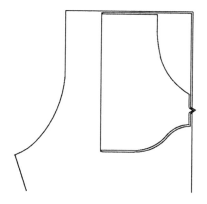

Cut two pockets from the fabric.

SEWING THE POCKETS

Pin a Pocket to each Front, matching the upper and side edges as illustrated.

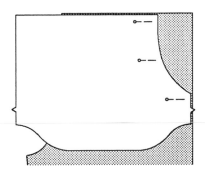

Trim the Front even with the Pocket.

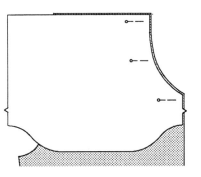

Stitch along the Pocket opening. Trim the seam allowances to ¼" (0.6 cm).

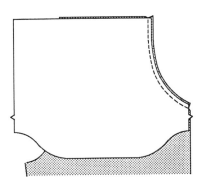

Press the seam open, where possible, for ease in turning. Press the Pocket to the wrong side of the garment, rolling the seam slightly to the underside.

Edgestitch the Pocket opening. Topstitch the Pocket opening 1″ (2.5 cm) from the edge.

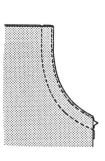

With right sides together, press the Pocket in half, matching the cut edges and the notches.

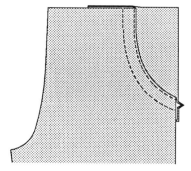

Pin the Pocket in the finished position.

Edgestitch and topstitch through all layers on the upper 2½″ (6.4 cm) of the Pocket opening, sewing over the previous stitching.

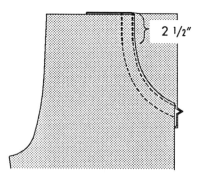

2 1/2″

Stitch the lower edges of the Pocket together.

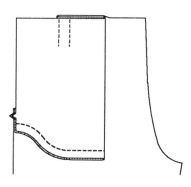

Machine baste the Pocket in place just inside the seamline on the side edge.

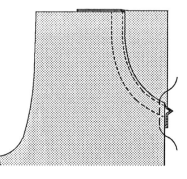

Machine baste the Pocket 1¾″ (4.4 cm) from the waist edge and trim both layers of the Pocket as illustrated.

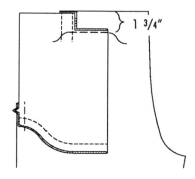

1 3/4″

❖❖❖❖❖

*W*hen hemming knits, take a tip from the designers. Use a 3mm-wide twin needle, size 80. Press in the hem and sew from the topside, using 3.5 to 4 stitch length. You may need to loosen top tension. Stitch about ⅛" from the turned-under raw edge, so the bobbin zigzags over it, eliminating the need to finish the raw edge first.

Our best-selling pattern is 5000 for adults and 5800 for children, because of its one-piece simplicity. It's easy to put together and great to embellish with pillow-panel overlays, continous serger flatlocking, or color blocking with leftover fabrics.

KATHIE KLEESE
STRETCH & SEW FABRICS
NILES, OH

❖❖❖

Side Seam Pockets

Pockets in a seam are easy to sew and can be added to any garment with a side seam. Remember to start with a pattern that has a turned-down 1¼" (3.2 cm) elastic waist.

❖

CUTTING THE POCKETS

To draw a pocket, use the grid illustration.

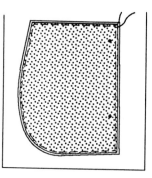

1 square = 1 inch (2.5 cm)

Cut four Pockets from the fabric. Transfer the dots to the Pockets. The dots mark the Pocket opening.

SEWING THE POCKETS

Place the upper edge of the Pocket 2″ (5.1 cm) from the waist edge of the pants, matching the cut edges at the side of the pants.

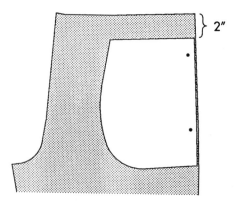

POCKET TIP:

If you're using a fabric that tends to stick to itself, keep the Pockets from sticking to the Fronts by cutting two Pockets from a silky lining fabric. With wrong sides together, machine baste the lining to a right and left Pocket close to the cut edges.

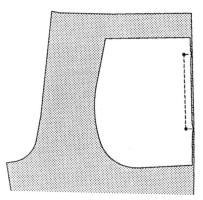

These Pockets will be treated as one layer and sewn to the Front. The pocket should finish with the lining against the wrong side of the Front.

Beginning at the side edge, stitch to the dot, pivot and continue stitching on the seamline to the other dot, pivot and stitch to the side edge.

Clip to the dots at an angle, being careful not to clip through the stitching.

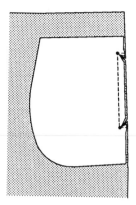

Press the seam open where possible, for ease in turning. Press the Pocket to the wrong side, rolling the seam slightly to the underside.

Topstitch around the Pocket opening at ¼″ (0.6 cm).

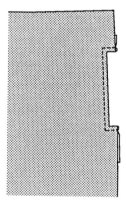

With right sides together, pin the remaining Pockets to each Pocket, matching the cut edges. Stitch around the Pockets from the side edge to the upper edge, being careful not to catch the Front in the stitching.

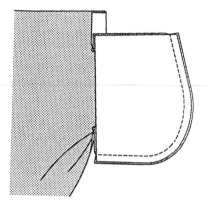

Machine baste the Pocket to the front at the upper edge of the pocket and at the side edge at ⅝″ (1.6 cm).

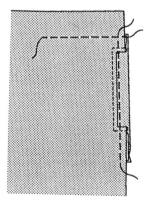

❖

No-Side-Seam Pockets

If you thought you couldn't add a pocket unless there was a side seam, you haven't tried this technique! Remember to start with a pattern that has a turned-down 1¼" (3.2 cm) elastic waist and no side seam in the pants leg.

CUTTING THE POCKETS

To draw a pocket, use the grid illustration.

Cut 2 Pockets from the fabric.

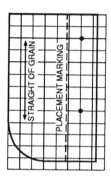

1 square = 1 inch (2.5 cm)

Transfer the dot markings to the Pockets. The dots indicate where your pocket opening will be.

SEWING THE POCKETS

Cut four pieces of woven fusible interfacing 1¼" wide by 8" long (3.2 by 20.3 cm). Draw a box ½" (1.3 cm) wide by 6" (15.7 cm) long down the center of each piece as illustrated.

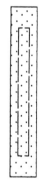

After cutting out the pants, mark the Pocket placement on the garment by folding the *right* pants leg in half and marking the center of the leg.

To mark the pocket openings on the pants, open up the pants leg. Place the Pocket *pattern piece* on the right side of the pants, matching the center leg marking on the pants to the Pocket placement marking and with the Pocket pattern piece 2″ (5.1 cm) down from the waist edge.

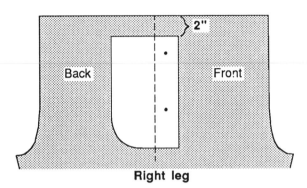

Right leg

Transfer the dots for the Pocket opening to the pants front.

NOTE:

The pocket is placed toward the back of the pants until you have stitched the opening. Then fold the pocket toward the front.

Flip the Pocket pattern piece and use the same procedure to mark the dots for the Pocket opening on the *left* pants leg.

Apply interfacing to the wrong side of the pants Fronts and Pockets, centering the ends of the box on the dots.

Serge or zigzag along the outer edges of each Pocket.

With right sides together, pin a Pocket to each Front/Back as illustrated, centering the ends of the box on the dots.

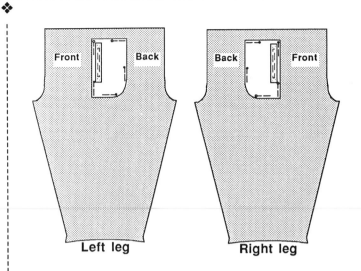

Left leg **Right leg**

Using a shorter stitch length, stitch around the box.

Cut on the cutting lines and clip into the corners, being careful not to clip through the stitching.

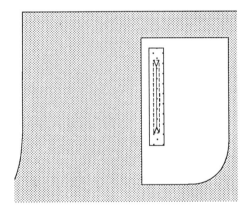

Turn the Pocket to the wrong side through the box and press the *front* edge of the Pocket, rolling the seam slightly to the underside.

Edgestitch along the front and ends of the Pocket opening.

❖

Topstitch at ¾" (1.9 cm) along the *front* Pocket opening.

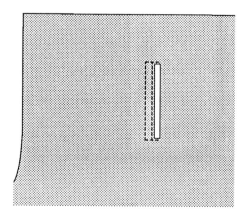

Fold the Pocket over the opening toward the center front and press.

Pin the Pocket in position. Machine baste across the top of the Pocket, close to the cut edge.

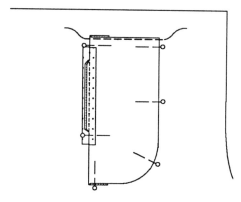

Stitch around the Pocket as illustrated, sewing next to the fold above and below the opening and ¼" (0.6 cm) from the cut edge on the remainder of the Pocket, extending the stitching to the waist edge of the pants.

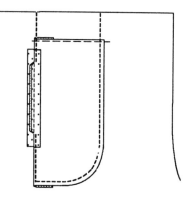

Bar-tack at the upper and lower edges of the Pocket opening.

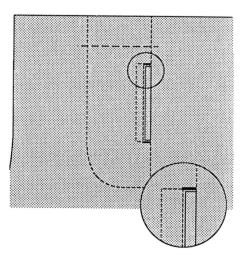

Sewing Pants

Basic Construction

SEWING THE SIDE SEAMS

With right sides together, stitch each side seam. (If you applied side seam pockets, follow the previous stitching line to avoid catching the opening in the stitching.)

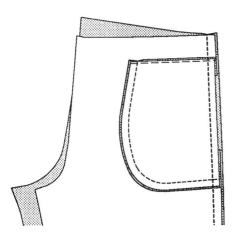

To keep the side seam flat, clip the *front* seam allowance only below the pocket. Press the seam allowance open below the clip and toward the back above the clip.

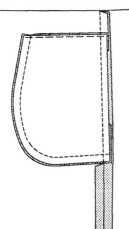

SEWING THE INSEAMS

Fold each leg right sides together and stitch the inside leg seams.

SEWING THE CROTCH SEAM

Turn one leg right side out and place it inside the other leg so that the right sides of the legs are together. Pin the crotch seam, matching the inside leg seams and waist edges. Stitch the crotch seam.

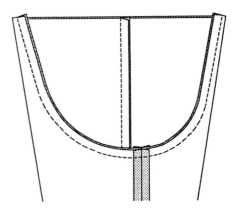

Doublestitch the crotch curve only. Trim the doublestitched portion of the seam by tapering to ¼″ (0.6 cm) in the crotch curve as illustrated.

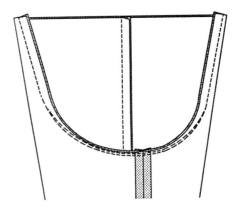

Press open the untrimmed portion of the seam.

TIP:

For sergers, if you want to reinforce the crotch, add a row of straight stitching *inside* the serged seam allowance.

❖

Choosing a Waist Finish

An elastic waistline provides comfort and fit. Here are two easy and attractive elastic waist finishes for you to try.

APPLYING ACTION ELASTIC

Action elastic, a special *Stretch & Sew* product, is used by many leading sportswear manufacturers and will give you that ready-to-wear look. The elastic is quick to apply—just stitch right through the elastic and it will not lose its elasticity.

This waist finish is comfortable for everything from activewear to evening wear. Your garment should extend 2½" (6.4 cm) above the waist to allow for this elastic application. After you have constructed the garment, follow these steps.

Preparing the Elastic

Cut one strip of 1¼"-wide (3.2 cm) action elastic 3" (7.6 cm) smaller than your waist measurement for sizes 32 to 38 and 5" (12.7 cm) smaller than your waist measurement for sizes 40 to 48.

Lap the ends of the elastic ½" (1.3 cm), forming a circle, and stitch securely.

Divide the elastic into fourths and mark with pins.

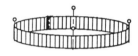

Divide the waist edge of the garment into fourths and mark with pins.

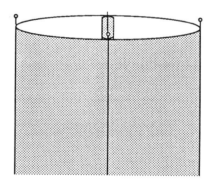

Pin the elastic to the wrong side of the garment at the waist edge, matching the quarter divisions.

❖

Adjusting for Stretch

If your fabric has more than 25-percent up-and-down stretch, you may need to adjust your crotch length.

Try on the garment, folding the elastic into the finished position as if sewn. If the crotch length seems long, measure the amount that is too long and trim that amount off the top edge of the garment. *Before trimming*, check to see if the Pocket opening will be affected. If the opening becomes too small, trim less.

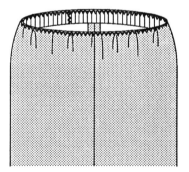

Repin the elastic to the garment and continue with the construction.

Sewing in the Elastic

With the elastic on top, serge or zigzag along the upper edge, stretching the elastic to fit. If desired, add a ribbon loop marking (see the box at right).

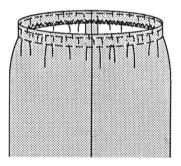

Fold the elastic to the wrong side of the garment so that the fabric encases the elastic. Then pin in position.

Using a long stitch and sewing on the inside of the garment, stitch along the lower edge of the elastic, keeping the elastic pulled taut equally in front and back of the needle. Sew another row of stitching ¼" (0.6 cm) from the upper edge of the garment, stretching as before.

RIBBON LOOP MARKING

For a handy way to mark the back of your pants, cut a strip of ribbon or twill tape 3½" (8.9 cm) long. Fold the strip in half and pin it in place at the center-back waist edge as illustrated.

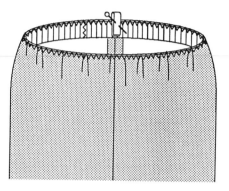

When you fold down the elastic for finishing, the loop will turn to the inside of the pants, marking the back. You won't have to give the pants a second look when you're hurriedly getting dressed on a busy morning.

To return the elastic to its original length, generously steam the waist area and, using your fingertips, carefully push the elastic back into shape as you steam.

❖

Applying Drawcord Elastic

This technique is great for pants that you may want to pull tighter at the waist. It is used especially in menswear and activewear.

Preparing the Elastic and Waistline

Cut one strip of 1¼"-wide (3.2 cm) action elastic 3" (7.6 cm) smaller than your waist measurement for sizes 32 to 38 and 5" (12.7 cm) smaller than your waist measurement for sizes 40 to 48.

Beginning ½" (1.3 cm) from each cut edge of the elastic, use a straight pin to pull the ends of the drawcord out approximately 5" (12.7 cm).

Lap the ends of the elastic ½" (1.3 cm), forming a circle, and stitch securely, being careful not to catch the cord in the stitching.

Divide the elastic into fourths, using the drawcord ties as the center front division, and mark with pins.

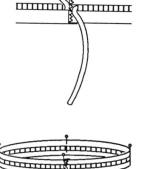

Machine stitch two ⅜" (1.0 cm) buttonholes ¼" (0.6 cm) from either side of the center front seam and ½" (1.3 cm) from the waist edge.

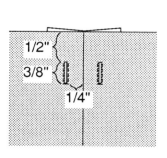

Divide the waist edge of the garment into fourths and mark with pins.

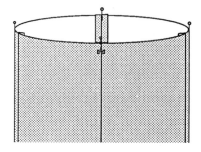

Pin the elastic to the wrong side of the garment at the waist edge, matching the quarter divisions. Pull the drawcord through the buttonholes and knot each end.

Sewing in the Elastic

With the elastic on top, serge or zigzag along the upper edge, stretching the elastic to fit.

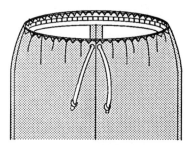

Fold the elastic to the wrong side of the garment so that the fabric encases the elastic. Then pin in position.

Sᴘᴏʀᴛ ʀᴇᴘᴏʀᴛ–ᴀᴄᴛɪᴠᴇᴡᴇᴀʀ ᴛʜᴀᴛ's ꜰɪᴛ ᴛᴏ ᴡᴇᴀʀ ᴀɴᴅ ᴇᴀsʏ ᴛᴏ sᴇᴡ.

DIVIDE & CONQUER—IT'S SO EASY TO APPLY ELASTIC THE *STRETCH & SEW* WAY.
FROM SWIMWEAR TO WAISTBANDS, YOU'LL BE AMAZED.

THE COMFORT ZONE: POCKETS IN PANTS. THERE ARE MANY CHOICES, SO YOU ALWAYS HAVE AN OPTION.

MAKE WAVES, GET RAVES WITH THE BEST-LOOKING, BEST-FITTING SWIMWEAR ON THE BEACH. SO EASY TO MAKE WITH *STRETCH & SEW*.

Sewing on the inside of the garment, stitch along the lower edge of the elastic, keeping the elastic pulled taut equally in front and back of the needle. Sew another row of stitching ¼" (0.6 cm) from the upper edge of the garment, stretching as before and being careful not to catch the cord in the stitching.

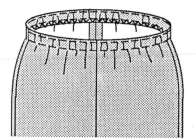

To return the elastic to its original length, generously steam the waist area and, using your fingertips, carefully push the elastic back into shape as you steam.

Finishing the Pants

HEMMING THE PANTS

Now you are ready to hem your pants. Pin in the hem at the lower edge of each leg, referring to your pattern instructions. Most pants will have a 1½" (3.8 cm) hem allowance. Try on the pants with the shoes you plan to wear with them. Adjust if necessary. Stitch the hem in place. See pages 20–23 for various methods of hemming.

PRESSING IN CREASES AFTER CONSTRUCTION

If you have waited to press creases in your pants until you were sure of the fit, place the pants on the ironing board and fold one leg out of the way. On the remaining leg, match the inside leg seam to the outside leg seam, following the lengthwise grain up the center front and center back of the pants leg. There will be a little extra fullness at the upper inside leg seam. Use a steam iron (wool setting) and a wet press cloth. Hold the iron firmly in one place until the press cloth is dry. Repeat until you have pressed a crease on the front and back from the lower edge to the crotch level.

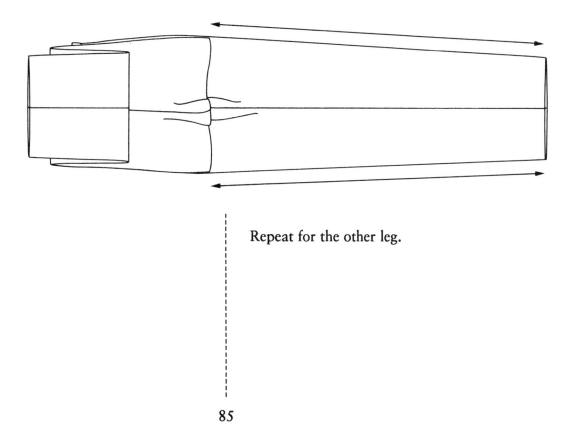

Repeat for the other leg.

Sewing Straight Skirts

Skirts are always classic and look great with jackets, sweaters, or tunics. For this garment, choose a pattern for a straight pull-on skirt that has a 1¼″ (3.2 cm) turned-down elastic waist.

Basic Construction

ADDING POCKETS

Of course any of the pockets you put on your pants you can also put on a skirt. Be sure you have enough room in the hip area to accommodate a pocket. Follow the same procedures to attach the pockets to your skirt front and then complete your skirt as follows.

❖

SEWING THE SIDE SEAMS

With right sides together, stitch each side seam.

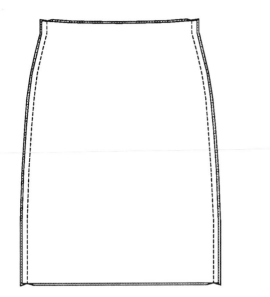

Press open the seam allowances. If pockets were added, refer to pag 81 for clipping and pressing procedures.

Try on the skirt. If a horizontal bubble appears at the center back, fold the skirt in half matching the side seams. At the waist edge, trim ¼ to ½" (0.6 cm to 1.3 cm) from the *center back*, tapering to the original cut edge at the side seams.

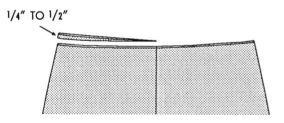

1/4" TO 1/2"

Now you are ready to finish the waist with one of the elastic techniques we discussed in pants. Refer to the waist finish you prefer.

❖❖❖❖❖

Ann's philosophy is "There has to be an easier way," and it is apparent in all her work. She makes every technique easy to do, with clear, easy-to-follow directions and patterns. I've had many customers comment, "Why can't all patterns be this easy?" Here are two tips our customers like:

1   *I like to incorporate ⅜"clear elastic in the shoulder seams when using very stretchy fabrics or heavier cotton sweaterings. Measure the pattern's shoulder seam length, not the cut fabric's shoulder length, and include the elastic in the seaming or serging. This keeps the shoulder seam from sagging.*

2   *After stitching Action Elastic onto the top of pants or skirts and turning it inside, I baste the quarter marks. Then when I stretch-and-sew, I don't have pins to contend with.*

My favorite pattern? Hands down, it has to be the sweatshirts. I use them as a base to create lots of different looks.

NANCY CORNWELL
STRETCH & SEW FABRICS/BERNINA
LYNNWOOD, WA

❖❖❖

Hemming the Skirt

Press in a 2″ (5.1 cm) hem at the lower edge of the garment. Try on the garment and adjust if necessary. Stitch the hem in place. Refer to pages 20–23 for various methods of hemming.

❖❖❖❖❖

I took my first Basic I series of Stretch & Sew classes more than 20 years ago. Before, I had played at sewing to stretch my budget, but was not very successful, as the patterns didn't fit or look good on my hard-to-fit size.

I was excited by the fun, simplicity, and speed with which a person could sew. It still looked professional and expensive. Sewing could be exciting, successful, and could fit any size person.

The past 22 years have been a real joy, watching students come to the same realizations: "It fits!" "The pieces mix and match so easily that I, too, can design things." "The instructions are so clear and easy to follow."

It has been a real privilege to work with someone the caliber of Ann Person. She is a very down-to-earth lady who can relate to people on any level. Her talent is difficult to match in the sewing industry. Because of her, sewing truly can be fast, fun, and easy, yet also fit and be fashionable.

JUDY CRAIG
STRETCH & SEW FABRICS/
SEW MUCH BETTER BERNINA
SALEM, OR

❖❖❖

5 SWIMWEAR, ACTIVEWEAR & LINGERIE

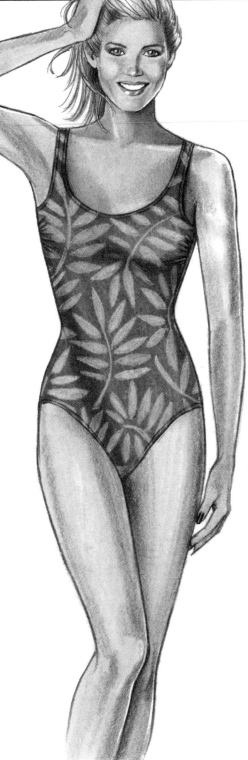

There isn't a garment I enjoy making more than a swimsuit. Both swimsuits and leotards take about one yard of fabric and an hour of your time—two reasons why they are my favorite garments to sew.

Basic Tank Swimsuit or Leotard

Activewear Fabrics

Both swimsuits and leotards need to be sewn from a Lycra-blend fabric to allow for the close fit and still have ease of movement. Lycra has great elasticity and excellent recovery even when blended with other fibers, such as cotton or nylon. And it is stronger and more durable than conventional elastic yarns and weighs a third less.

All Lycra-blend fabrics are sensitive to saltwater, and prolonged exposure to sun and chlorine will cause the fabric to fade. Rinse your swimsuit in fresh water and line-dry in the shade after each wearing.

Nylon/Lycra and cotton/Lycra fabrics have different characteristics.

COTTON/LYCRA

Cotton/Lycra fabric is soft and comfortable. It is used extensively for exercisewear but can be used for swimwear as well. Because cotton is a natural fiber, cotton/Lycra will wear faster and has a tendency to sun fade. Cotton/Lycra should be pretreated by gently washing in cool water and line drying.

LINING FABRIC

When dry, all swim fabric is opaque. Dark colors or closely spaced prints with dark backgrounds remain opaque wet or dry, but lighter shades of solid colors and prints may become transparent when wet. Therefore, you may want to line the front of a swimsuit made from a light color. Choose a lining specifically manufactured for swimwear that has the same stretch as your swim fabric. With white swim fabric, you can even use self-fabric for the lining. You will not be able to see through the suit, plus the extra layer of fabric adds stability and helps smooth your figure.

Overall Body Measurement

Besides taking your bust, waist, and hip measurements, you will want to take an *overall body measurement* to be sure your one-piece swimsuit or leotard fits you in length. This is an awkward measurement to take yourself, so I suggest you have someone else do it to ensure the greatest possible accuracy. Take the measurement from the hollow at the front natural neckline, down through the crotch, and up to the cervical bone at the back of the natural neckline. Keep the tape measure snug against your body.

NYLON/LYCRA

Nylon/Lycra fabric is excellent for swimwear. Because nylon is a synthetic, the fiber is very strong and will wear well. Nylon fabrics are bright and bold with a silken luster and hold their color. Nylon/Lycra has excellent memory and will snap back into shape after being stretched. It is also a good choice for exercisewear. Nylon/Lycra fabric does not need to be pretreated.

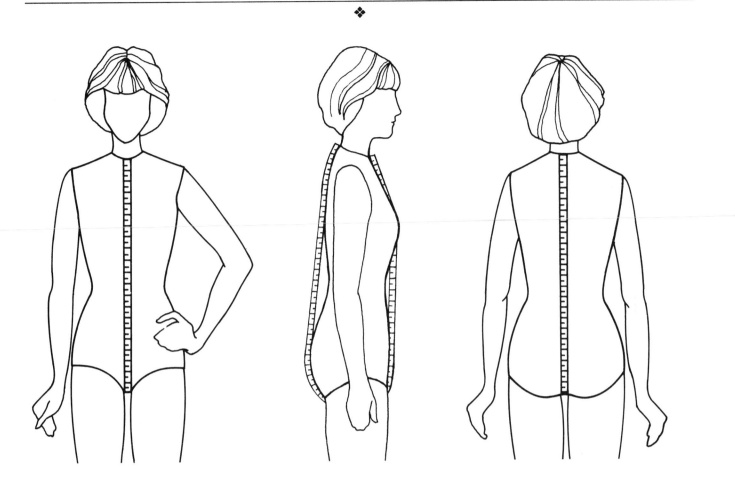

Compare your overall body measurement to the chart below:

STRETCH & SEW OVERALL BODY MEASUREMENT

Bust Size	Inches	Centimeters
30	53	134.6
32	54	137.2
34	55	139.7
36	56	142.2
38	57	144.8
40	58	147.3
42	59	149.9
44	60	152.4
46	60 3/4	154.3

LENGTH ADJUSTMENT

If your overall measurement is the same as that on the overall body measurement chart, your swimsuit pattern does not need to be adjusted for length.

If the measurement is not the same, you must shorten or lengthen the pattern pieces. Adjust the pattern pieces by *half* of the difference between the measurements to account for the stretch of the fabric.

So, take *half* the difference between measurements and divide into fourths. Then adjust all appropriate pattern pieces this amount on each shorten/lengthen line.

❖

Example of Shortening

For example, if your own overall body measurement is 53″ (134.6 cm) and the chart measurement for your size is 55″ (139.7 cm), your own measurement is 2″ (5.1 cm) less. Take half of this amount, or 1″ (2.5 cm), out of your pattern.

Because there are four shorten/lengthen lines, two on the Front and two on the Back, divide the 1″ (2.5 cm) into fourths to get ¼″ (0.6 cm) at each line.

Slash and spread the Front and Back pattern pieces ¼″ (0.6 cm) at each shorten/lengthen line and back the openings with strips of tracing paper. You have added a total of 1″ (2.5 cm) to your pattern.

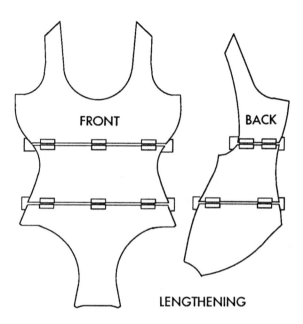

LENGTHENING

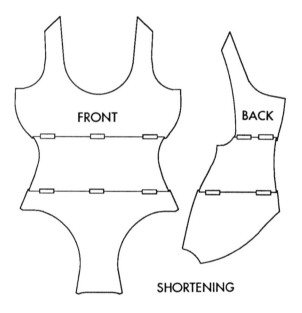

SHORTENING

Example of Lengthening

Or, if your own overall body measurement is 58″ (147.3 cm) and the chart measurement for your size is 56″ (142.2 cm), your own measurement would be 2″ (5.1 cm) greater. Add half of this amount, or 1″ (2.5 cm), to your pattern.

Because there are four shorten/lengthen lines, two on the Front and two on the Back, divide the 1″ (2.5 cm) into fourths to get ¼″ (0.6 cm) at each line.

Pattern Layout

With a little thought and planning *before* you cut your garment, you can create a great-looking swimsuit. When working with prints or stripes, play with the positioning of the pattern pieces before cutting to be sure you like the look.

Below are some of the basic guidelines for laying out your pattern pieces.

LENGTHWISE VERSUS CROSSWISE GRAIN

Nylon/Lycra fabric has the greater stretch on the *lengthwise* grain. Cotton/Lycra fabric has the greater stretch on the *crosswise* grain. Regardless of the type of fabric you choose, the greater amount of stretch must go across the pattern pieces—*around the body in the finished garment.*

❖

To cut the pattern pieces from a *single* thickness of fabric, open the fabric out flat, being sure to position the pieces so that the greater stretch goes around the body in the finished garment.

To cut the pattern pieces from a *double* thickness of fabric, fold the fabric as illustrated, being sure the greater stretch goes around the body in the finished garment.

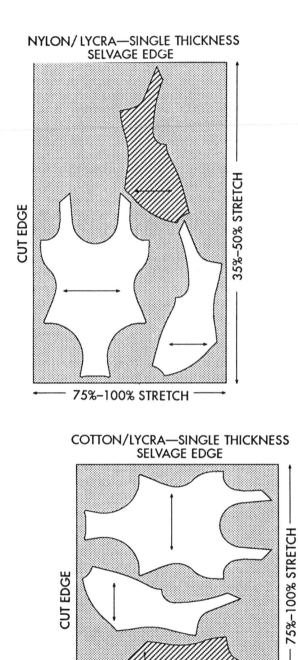

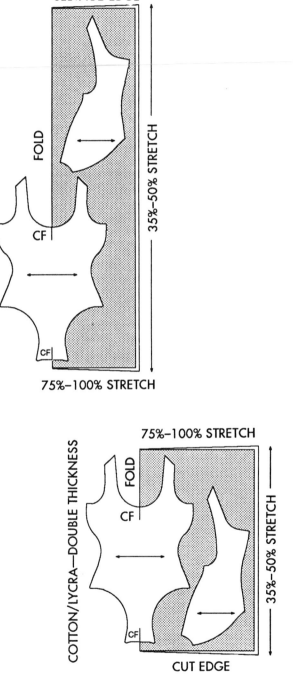

❖

Remember these steps when laying out your pattern:

• When cutting pattern pieces from a single thickness, cut one piece, then turn pattern over to cut the second piece. This will give you a right side and left side.

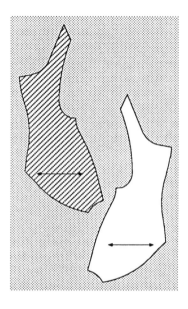

• Cut notches outward or use a fabric marker to indicate the notches. Clipping into the fabric to mark the notches will weaken the seam.

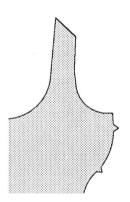

• Transfer all construction marks to your fabric and lining.
• Elastic will be cut during construction.

Swimsuit Basic Construction

With right sides together, stitch the center back seam. This is a stress seam, so be sure to doublestitch if you are not serging.

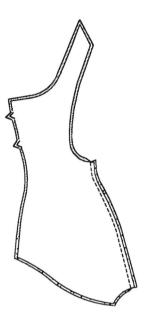

With right sides together, stitch the Front to the Back at the crotch seam.

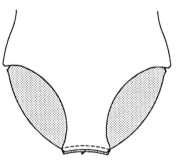

❖

For the swimsuit only: Pin the right side of the Crotch Lining over the wrong side of the Back. Stitch on the seam allowance next to the previous stitching.

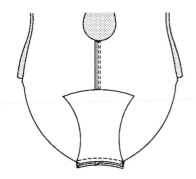

Fold the Crotch Lining to the Front, enclosing the seam allowances. Pin the Crotch Lining even with the leg openings. Machine baste ⅜" (1.0 cm) from the cut edge.

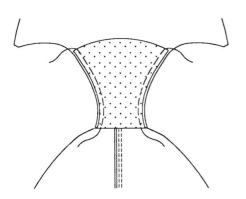

Trim the lining only, close to the stitching.

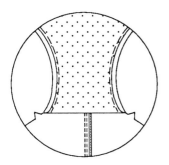

If your pattern has bust gathers, machine baste at ⅛" and ⅜" (0.3 and 1.0 cm) between the notches on the Front.

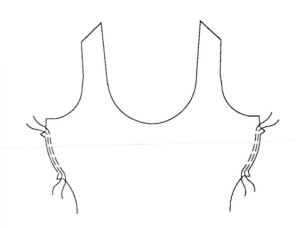

Stitch the Front to the Back at each side seam. If your pattern has bust gathers, match the notches and pull the gathers to fit before stitching.

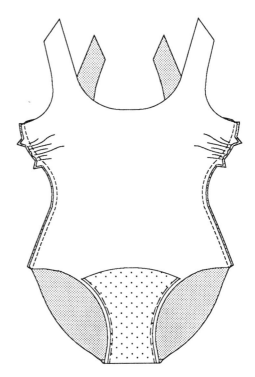

Stitch each shoulder seam, matching the cut edges at the ¼″ (0.6 cm) seamlines, as illustrated. The shoulder seams often are bias-cut to reduce bulk.

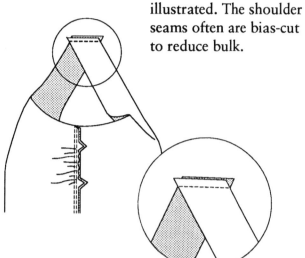

Leotard Basic Construction

Stitch shoulder seams.

For a leotard with sleeves, stitch each sleeve to garment, streching to fit.

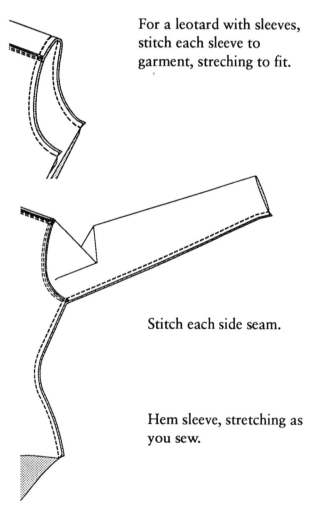

Stitch each side seam.

Hem sleeve, stretching as you sew.

Elastic Application

Keep in mind that elastic is used to keep your swimsuit and leotard in place, not to pull the suit in to fit you.

APPLYING THE LEG ELASTIC

Cut two strips of ⅜″ (1.0 cm) elastic, referring to the appropriate chart in your *Stretch & Sew* pattern. This measurement is 1:1 with the cut edge in the front, and two-thirds the measurement across the back.

Lap the ends of each strip of elastic ½″ (1.3 cm), forming a circle, and stitch securely.

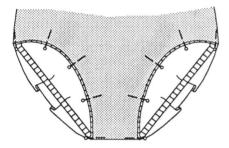

With the garment right side out, pin the elastic to the wrong side of the garment even with the cut edge so that the elastic is a 1:1 ratio along the front leg opening from the crotch seam to the side seam and the rest is stretched across the back leg opening. Place the overlap just past the crotch seam on the back leg.

With the elastic on top and the garment against the feed dog of machine, serge or zigzag the elastic close to the cut edge, stretching the elastic evenly across the back leg opening. Make sure that the stitching encloses the edge of the elastic.

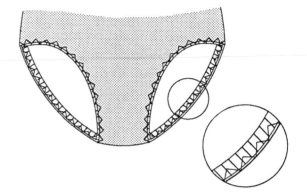

❖❖❖❖❖

We find the Stretch & Sew patterns to be the best for fit, consistency in directions, more pictures than words, and always fashionable. My favorite patterns are the T-Shirt and No-Side-Seam Pants for beginners; Pull-on Pants for intermediate students; and the Blazer Cardigan for a most versatile jacket.

PAT HEADEN
HARTSDALE FABRICS
HARTSDALE, NY

❖❖❖

❖

Fold the elastic to the wrong side of the leg, enclosing the elastic. Stitch a second time as close to the edge as possible. Stitching may be done with a long straight stitch or a double-needle or zigzag stitch. Stretch the elastic as you sew.

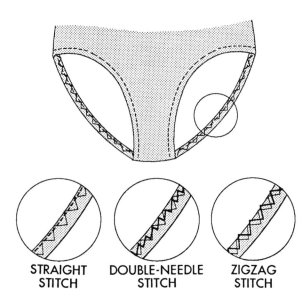

STRAIGHT STITCH   DOUBLE-NEEDLE STITCH   ZIGZAG STITCH

Sewing close to the raw edge will prevent the elastic from rolling out when you wear the suit. Zigzag and double-needle stitches provide some built-in stretch, so it is not necessary to stretch as firmly with these stitches.

APPLYING THE NECK ELASTIC

For a leotard with a high back: Cut one strip of ⅜" (1.0 cm) elastic the measurement of the neck opening at the cut edge plus ½" (1.3 cm) for overlap.

For a swimsuit with a low back: Cut one strip of ⅜" (1.0 cm) elastic the measurement of the neck opening at the cut edge minus 2" (5.1 cm).

Lap the ends of the elastic ½" (1.3 cm), forming a circle, and stitch securely. Divide the elastic into fourths and mark the divisions with pins.

Divide the neckline of the garment into fourths and mark the divisions with pins. The quarter marks will not fall at the shoulder seams.

With the garment right side out, pin the neckline elastic to the wrong side of the garment, even with the cut edge, matching the quarter divisions and placing the overlap in the shoulder area.

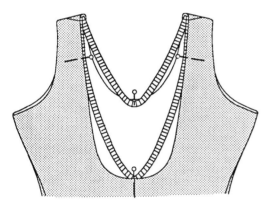

With the elastic on top and the garment against the feed dog of the machine, serge or zigzag the elastic close to the cut edge, stretching the elastic to fit where necessary. Make sure the stitching encloses the edge of the elastic.

APPLYING THE ARMHOLE ELASTIC

Cut two strips of ⅜" (1.0 cm) elastic the measurement of the armhole at the cut edge plus ½" (1.3 cm) for overlap.

❖

Lap the ends of the elastic ½″ (1.3 cm), forming a circle, and stitch securely. Divide the elastic into fourths and mark the divisions with pins.

Divide each armhole into fourths and mark the divisions with pins.

With the garment right side out, pin the armhole elastic to the wrong side of the garment, even with the cut edge, matching the quarter divisions.

With the elastic on top and the garment against the feed dog of the machine, serge or zigzag the elastic close to the cut edge, stretching the elastic to fit. Make sure the stitching encloses the edge of the elastic.

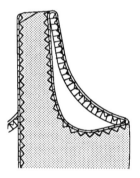

Using the same procedures as you did for the leg elastic on page 98, fold the elastic to the wrong side of the neck and armhole so that the fabric will enclose the elastic. Stitch along the inside edge of the elastic, using a long, straight stitch or a double-needle or zigzag stitch.

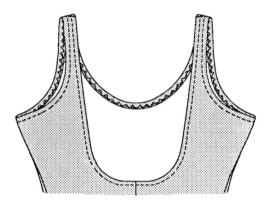

Bandeaus and Bra-Cup Linings

You will find that the finest ready-to-wear swimsuits have front linings or bandeaus made from swim lining fabric. Both can be constructed with or without bra cups. Sewing your own swimsuit really does let you personalize your garment!

CONSTRUCTING A SUIT WITH A BANDEAU

Begin constructing your swimsuit using the procedures described in Basic Construction on pages 94–95, and sew the following:

- Center back seam
- Crotch seam and lining
- Side bust gathers
- Side seams

If your swimsuit pattern does not have a bandeau, make one using the front of your swimsuit pattern. Just decide how long you want your bandeau to be, draw a horizontal line across the Front pattern piece at that length, and cut the bandeau based on the drawn line.

❖

Cut Bandeau from swim lining.

On the curved lower edge of the Bandeau, machine baste at ⅛″ and ⅜″ (0.3 and 1.0 cm) on each side.

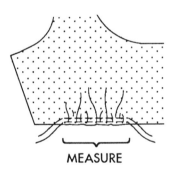

Pull the gathers up so that each side measures according to the chart below.

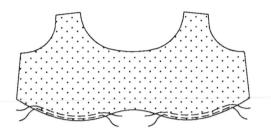

MEASURE

BANDEAU GATHERING CHART

Size	Inches	Centimeters
30	3	7.6
32	3¼	8.3
34	3½	8.9
36	3⅝	9.2
38	3¾	9.5
40	4	10.2
42	4¼	10.8
44	4½	11.4
46	4⅝	11.7

Applying the Elastic

Cut one strip of ¾″ (1.9 cm) *felt-back* elastic the measurement of the bandeau's lower edge after it is gathered.

Divide the elastic and the lower edge of the Bandeau in half and mark the divisions with pins.

Matching the divisions and the cut edges of the elastic to the sides, pin the nonfelted side of the elastic to the right side of the Bandeau, overlapping ⅜″ (1.0 cm).

Zigzag along the upper edge of the elastic.

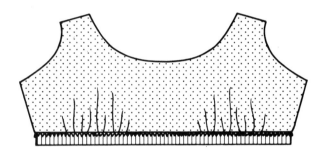

❖

Sewing in the Bandeau

With *wrong* sides together, pin the Bandeau to the Front along the side and upper edges. Stitch on the seam allowance next to the previous stitching at the side seams. Machine baste ⅜" (1.0 cm) from the edge at the neck and armholes.

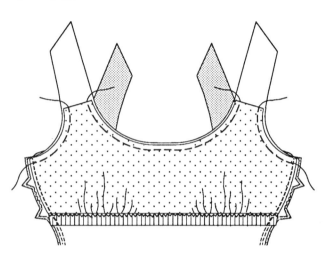

Trim the Bandeau only, close to the stitching at the neck and armholes.

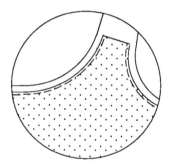

Completing the Garment

Stitch each shoulder seam, matching the cut edges at the ¼" (0.6 cm) seamlines as illustrated. The shoulder seams often are bias-cut to reduce bulk.

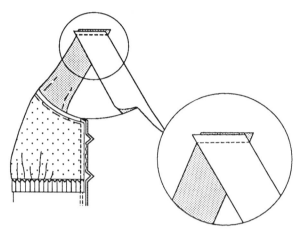

CONSTRUCTING A SWIMSUIT WITH A BRA-CUP LINING

Sew your swimsuit as directed on page 100, but before applying the elastic, add a bandeau with bra cups. Use purchased bra cups that can be sewn into your bra-lining piece cut from swim lining.

Sewing Bra Cups into the Lining

Place the inside of the bra cups (the side that will be against your body) on the wrong side of the Bra-Cup Lining, placing the high point of the cup directly over the high point mark on the Bra-Cup Lining. Bra cups need to be positioned at least ¾" (1.9 cm) away from the neck edge and slightly apart at the center front.

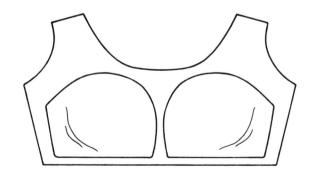

❖

Pin the bra cups in place. Hold the bra cups against your body and adjust the separation if necessary.

TIP:

When pinning the bra cups to the Bra-Cup Lining, do not flatten out the cups; keep them in the same shape as if they were on your body. The Bra-Cup Lining should lie flat and smooth under the cups.

Zigzag around the edges of the cups. Trim the Bra-Cup Lining from the inside cups, close to the stitching.

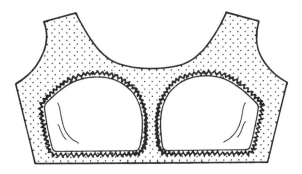

Applying the Elastic

Cut one strip of ¾" (1.9 cm) felt-back elastic the measurement of the lower edge of the bra lining minus 2" (5.1 cm).

Divide the elastic and the lower edge of the Bra-Cup Lining in half and mark the divisions with pins.

Matching the divisions and cut edges of the elastic to sides, pin the nonfelt side of the elastic to the right side of the Bra-Cup Lining, overlapping ⅜" (1.0 cm).

Zigzag along the upper edge of the elastic, stretching the elastic to fit.

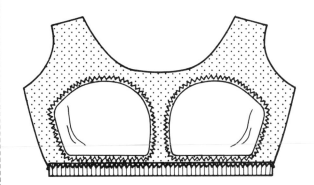

Sewing in the Bra-Cup Lining

With wrong sides together, pin the Bra-Cup Lining to the Front along the side and upper edges. Stitch on the seam allowance next to the previous stitching at the side seams. Machine baste ⅜" (1.0 cm) from the cut edge at the neck and armholes.

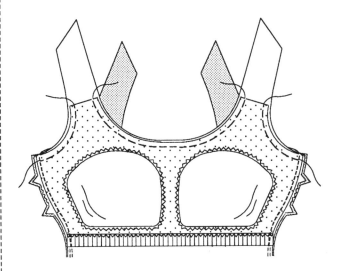

Trim the Bra-Cup Lining only, close to the stitching at the neck and armhole.

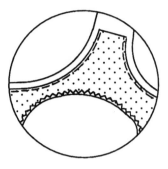

Stitch each shoulder seam, matching the cut edges at the ¼" (0.6 cm) seamlines, as illustrated. The shoulder seams are bias-cut to reduce bulk.

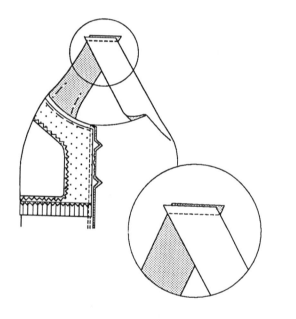

Exercise Separates

Exercise—it's a way of life. As you bend, stretch, run, and jump your way to a healthy life and a great body, you'll want to be comfortable and look good. Routine workouts don't have to mean routine work-out wear. Cotton/Lycra is ideal for exercisewear. The cotton is absorbent and the Lycra keeps your garment form-fitting and comfortable. Don't be afraid to add individuality. Details make all the difference.

No sweat—you'll be lookin' good and feelin' alive in the most energetic-looking sportswear around. So, come on and get physical!

❖

Tank-Style Bra Top

Get serious about a tank top. This cropped tank-style bra top will have you in top form in no time.

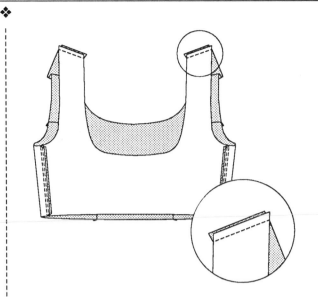

CONSTRUCTING THE TOP

Stitch each side seam and shoulder seam, matching the cut edges at the ¼″ (0.6 cm) seamlines as illustrated.

CUTTING THE NECK AND ARMHOLE ELASTIC

For the neck, cut one strip of ⅜″-wide (1.0 cm) elastic so that it measures 1:1 with the cut edge of the neck plus ½″ (1.3 cm) for overlap.

For the armhole, cut two strips of ⅜″-wide (1.0 cm) elastic so that it measures 1:1 with the cut edge of the armhole plus ½″ (1.3 cm) for overlap.

On *each* strip of elastic, lap the ends ½″ (1.3 cm), forming a circle, and stitch securely. Divide the elastic into fourths and mark with pins.

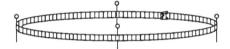

❖

APPLYING THE NECK AND ARMHOLE ELASTIC

Divide the neckline of the garment into fourths and mark with pins. Quarter divisions may not fall at shoulder seams.

With the garment right side out, pin the neckline elastic to the wrong side of the garment even with the cut edge, matching the quarter divisions and placing the overlap in the shoulder area.

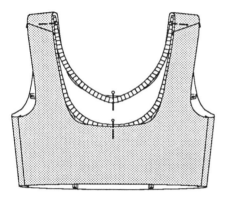

With the elastic on top and the garment against the feed dog of the machine, serge or zigzag the elastic close to the cut edge. Be sure the stitching encloses the edge of the elastic.

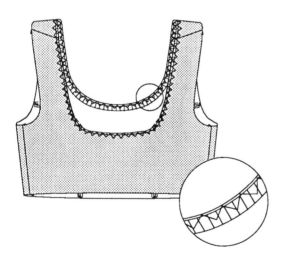

Divide each armhole into fourths and mark with pins.

Pin the armhole elastic to the wrong side of the garment, even with the cut edges and matching the quarter divisions.

Serge or zigzag the elastic to the garment.

Fold the elastic to the wrong side of the neck and armhole, so that the fabric encloses the elastic. Stitch along the inside edge of the elastic, using a long straight stitch, double needle, or zigzag.

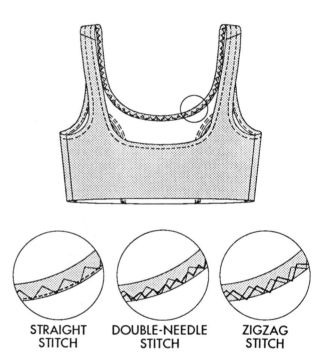

STRAIGHT STITCH   DOUBLE-NEEDLE STITCH   ZIGZAG STITCH

❖

FINISHING THE LOWER EDGE

Choose one of the following two methods to
finish the lower edge.

Applying Elastic to the Lower Edge

Cut one strip of ¾″-wide (1.9 cm) elastic so that
the measurement is 1:1 with the cut edge plus
½″ (1.3 cm) for overlap.

Lap the ends of the elastic ½″ (1.3 cm), forming
a circle, and stitch securely. Divide the elastic
into fourths and mark with pins.

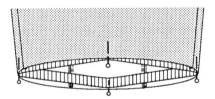

Divide the lower edge of the garment into
fourths and mark with pins. Quarter divisions
may not fall at shoulder seams.

With the garment right side out, pin the elastic
to the wrong side of the garment even with the
cut edge and matching the pins.

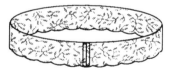

Apply midriff elastic, referring to the procedures
used for neckline and armhole elastic on pages
105–106.

Applying Stretch Lace to the Lower Edge

Here's a nice alternative to the elastic finish.

Trim ¾″ (1.9 cm) from the lower edge.

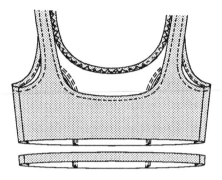

Cut one strip of 2″-wide (5.1 cm) stretch lace so
that the measurement is 1:1 with the cut edge
plus ½″ (1.3 cm) for the seam allowance.

With right sides together, sew the ends of the
stretch lace with a ¼″ (0.6 cm) seam allowance,
forming a circle. Finger-press the seam open.

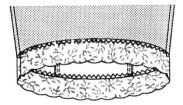

With right sides up, pin the stretch lace to the
lower edge of the garment, placing the seam in
the lace at the side seam and overlapping the
lace ¼″ (0.6 cm). Stitch with a narrow zigzag.

Exercise Shorts

Hot exercise shorts are true to form to match your every curve.

CONSTRUCTING THE SHORTS

Stitch each inseam.

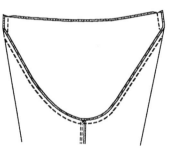

Turn one leg right side out and place it inside the other leg so that the right sides of the legs are together. Stitch the crotch seam, matching the inside leg seams and waist edges.

For sergers, if you want to reinforce the crotch, add a row of straight stitching *inside* the serged seam allowance.

APPLYING THE ELASTIC

Cut one strip of 1¼″-wide (3.2 cm) action elastic, 3″ (7.6 cm) smaller than your waist measurement for sizes 32 to 38 and 5″ (12.7 cm) smaller for sizes 40 to 48.

To apply waist elastic, refer to the procedures for Pants in Chapter 4 on pages 82–83.

COTTON/LYCRA ADJUSTMENT

If your fabric has more than 25-percent up-and-down stretch, you may want to try on the garment to see if you need to trim it at the upper edge before stitching the elastic.

With the elastic pinned in place at the upper edge, try on the garment, folding the elastic into the finished position as if sewn. If the crotch length seems long, measure the amount that is too long and trim that amount off the top edge of the garment.

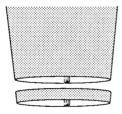

Repin the elastic and continue constructing the garment.

FINISHING THE LOWER EDGE

Choose one of the following two methods to finish the lower edge.

Hemming the Lower Edge

Turn up a ¾″ (1.9 cm) hem at the lower edge of each leg. Stitch in place using a single or double needle and stretching firmly as you sew.

Adding Stretch Lace to the Lower Edge

Trim ¾″ (1.9 cm) from the lower edge of each leg.

Cut two strips of 2″-wide (5.1 cm) stretch lace so that the measurement is 1:1 with the cut edge plus ½″ (1.3 cm) for the seam allowance.

With right sides together, sew the ends of the stretch lace with a ¼″ (0.6 cm) seam allowance, forming a circle. Finger-press the seam open.

With right sides up, pin the stretch lace to the lower edge of the garment, matching the seams and overlapping the lace ¼″ (0.6 cm). Stitch with a narrow zigzag.

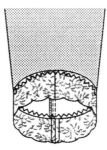

❖

Lingerie: Panties, Camisoles, and Slips

For keeping or gift-giving, home-sewn "under-fashion basics" are a wonderful treat.

There are many wonderful lingerie fabrics on the market today. You can choose from 100-percent cotton jerseys or cotton/Lycra blends to nylon tricot and all-over stretch laces.

A NOTE ON LINGERIE SEAMS:

Lingerie seam finishes must be delicate enough to accommodate the lingerie fabrics you use, yet sturdy enough to hold up against frequent launderings. The finish you choose will depend on your garment style, fabric type and weight, and the amount of wear and care. But make it a habit to finish seam edges wherever appropriate.

Elastic Application: Four Options

Choose from four basic elastic application methods and use them interchangeably on most lingerie garments. You may find you prefer using one method for all your garments, or you may use different methods for different purposes.

Quality elastic is an important consideration when sewing lingerie. When choosing elastic, you'll want elastic especially made for lingerie. It's lighter in weight, which eliminates bulk, comes in a variety of colors, and has a pretty edge to complement delicate garments.

Lingerie elastic must have the elasticity and recovery needed to be stitched through and still return to its original shape. Use ¼" (0.6 cm) or ⅜" (1.0 cm) *lingerie* elastic with these applications.

METHOD 1: EXPOSED ELASTIC

This method, with the elastic turned to the outside, is the one referred to most frequently in this chapter.

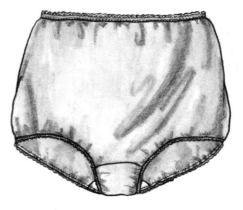

Cut a strip of elastic 4" to 6" (10.2 to 15.2 cm) less than your waist measurement. Sew the ends of the elastic together with a ¼" (0.6 cm) seam allowance, forming a circle. Finger-press the seam open.

❖

Divide the elastic and the garment into fourths and mark the divisions with pins.

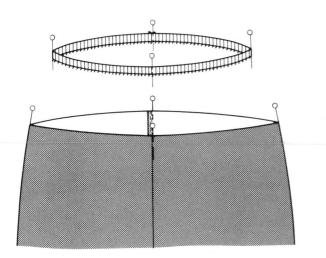

At this point, you can add a ribbon splice to cover the joined ends of the elastic if desired. Refer to page 113.

With the straight edge of the elastic even with the cut edge of the garment, pin the elastic to the garment with the wrong sides together, matching the quarter divisions.

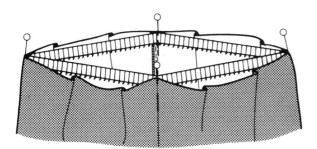

With the elastic on top and the garment next to the sewing machine, use a narrow zigzag stitch to sew the elastic to the garment along the picot edge, stretching the elastic to fit the garment.

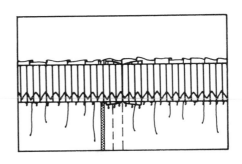

Trim the garment seam allowance close to the stitching. Turn the elastic to the right side of the garment and zigzag again, along the lower edge.

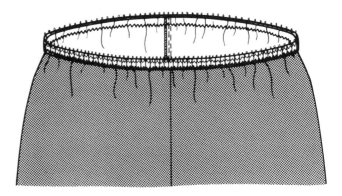

To return the elastic to its original length, generously steam the waist area and, using your fingertips, carefully push the elastic back into shape as you steam.

❖

METHOD 2: ELASTIC TURNED TO THE INSIDE

This application is similar to Method 1, except the elastic is turned to the inside of the garment.

Sew the ends of the elastic together with a ¼" (0.6 cm) seam allowance, forming a circle. Finger-press the seam open.

Divide the elastic and garment into fourths and mark the divisions with pins.

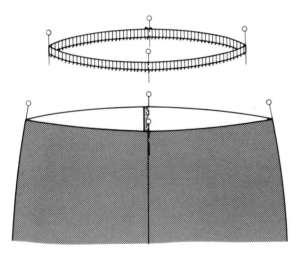

At this point, you can add a ribbon splice to cover the joined ends of the elastic if desired. Refer to page 113.

With the straight edge of the elastic even with the waist edge, pin the elastic to the garment with the right sides together, matching the quarter divisions.

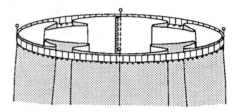

With the elastic on top and the garment next to the sewing machine, use a narrow zigzag stitch to sew the elastic to the garment along the picot edge, stretching the elastic to fit the garment.

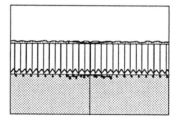

Trim the garment seam allowance close to the stitching. Turn the elastic to the wrong side of the garment and zigzag along the the lower edge, or topstitch with a double needle to finish.

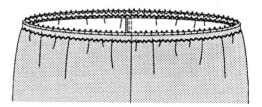

❖

ADDING A RIBBON SPLICE

The ribbon splice is an easy technique that adds a professional touch to the exposed elastic applications. The ribbon splice covers the joined ends of elastic and gives a finished appearance.

Cut a strip of ½″-wide (1.3 cm) satin ribbon 3″ (7.6 cm) long for each splice.

For exposed elastic, pin the right side of the ribbon to the wrong side of the garment at the center back, lining up the cut edge of the ribbon with the waist edge.

For elastic turned to the inside, pin the right side of the ribbon to the right side of the garment at the center back, lining up the cut edge of the ribbon with the waist edge.

Note: The illustrations show the exposed elastic application.

Pin the elastic to the garment following the instructions for the desired elastic application, placing the seam of the elastic over the ribbon.

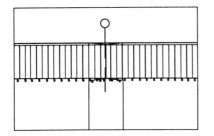

After sewing the elastic to the garment, trim the garment and the ribbon seam allowance ⅛″ (0.3 cm) from the stitching. Wrap the ribbon over the elastic edge to the other side of the garment. Trim off the excess ribbon as illustrated.

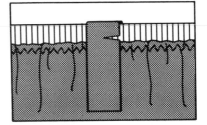

Tuck the end of the ribbon under the elastic and pin.

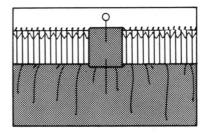

Zigzag along the lower edge, or topstitch with a double needle to finish.

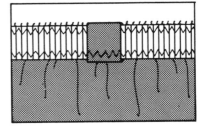

METHOD 3:
STRETCH LACE INSTEAD OF ELASTIC

Try using stretch lace in place of waist or leg elastic for an attractive finish that is comfortable to wear and smooth under your garments.

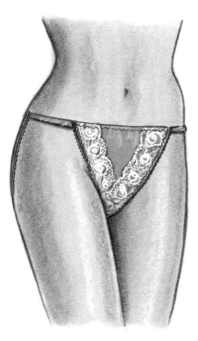

For the waist, use ⅔ the measurement of the panty upper-edge opening plus ½″ (1.3 cm). For the legs, use ⅔ the measurement of the panty leg opening plus ½″ (1.3 cm).

Sew the ends of the stretch lace together with a ¼″ (0.6 cm) seam allowance, forming a circle. Finger-press the seam open.

Divide the stretch lace and the garment opening into fourths and mark the divisions with pins.

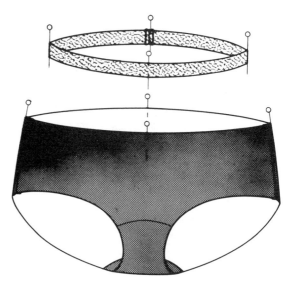

With the wrong side of the lace against the right side of the garment, pin the stretch lace to the garment opening, matching the upper edges and quarter divisions.

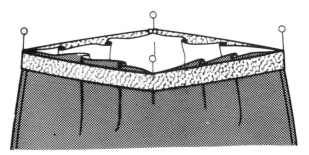

Using a narrow zigzag stitch, sew the lace to the garment along the lower edge of the lace, stretching the lace to fit the garment. Trim away the fabric behind the lace close to the stitching.

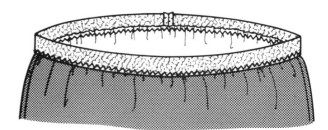

METHOD 4: FLATLOCK STITCHING

You can use this serger method to apply stretch lace or elastic to your garment.

Set your serger for a flatlock stitch, following your owner's manual.

With right sides together and matching the edge of the lace or elastic to the cut edge of the garment, serge, stretching the elastic to fit.

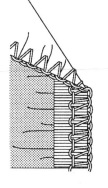

Once you have serged the lace or elastic, gently pull the lace or elastic and fabric out flat and the seam will lie flat also.

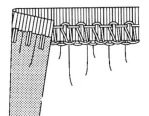

Full Panty

Give yourself a treat! Fill a dresser drawer with customized panties in your favorite colors and designs, all made especially and exclusively for you!

No matter what your favorite panty style is, you can make it. You can sew a pair of panties to match a new slip. Where you want lace, you can add lace. For comfort, add a crotch lining from 100-percent cotton.

Constructing the Panty

Matching the center front notches, sandwich the panty Front between the right sides of both Crotch pieces and pin.

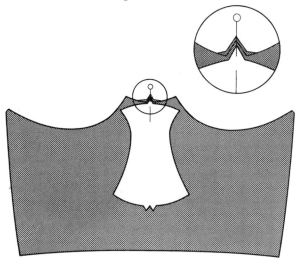

Match the ends of the Crotches to the Front and pin. Stitch through all thicknesses.

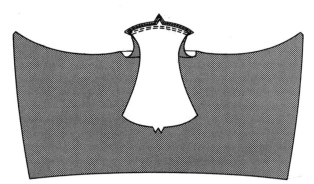

Fold the Crotches down over the seam and press.

Place the right side of the back Crotch on the right side of the Back, matching the center notches and side edges and pin.

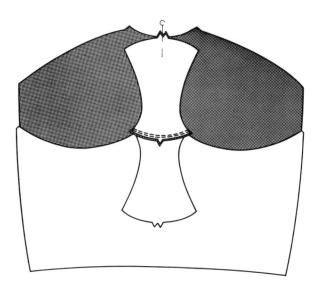

To enclose the back crotch seam, bring the remaining Crotch piece under and around the panty, matching the back notches as illustrated. Stitch the Crotches and the Back together through all thicknesses. Doublestitch.

Trim the notches on the seam allowances

Turn right side out and press.

Beginning at the lower edge, stitch each side seam.

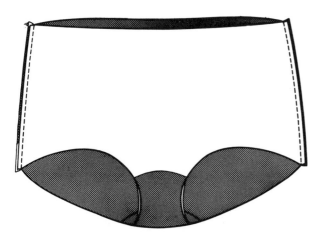

APPLYING THE ELASTIC

Apply elastic or stretch lace to the legholes and waist using one of the methods described on pages 110–115.

❖❖❖❖❖

*A*t Eunice Farmer Fabrics, we have always featured high-end natural fiber and imported designer fabrics. We are probably the least likely fabric shop to feature Stretch & Sew. But since Stretch & Sew had not been in our area for many years, we decided to give it a try to see if there was still interest. We were astounded with our seminar and class registrations. Our initial seminar drew 260 women, who paid $10 each.

Stretch & Sew encourages using wovens as well as knits and often a combination of both. It is a perfect bridge between today's unconstructed fashions and the limited amount of time available for today's busy women to sew. Everyone loves it and I see a bright future for Stretch & Sew in St. Louis.

EUNICE FARMER
EUNICE FARMER FABRICS, INC.
ST. LOUIS, MO

❖❖❖

❖

Full Slip and Camisole

Treat yourself to just the right fit and great feel underneath clothing. These garments involve the same construction steps, but one is longer than the other.

CONSTRUCTING THE SLIP OR CAMISOLE

Stitch the center back seam.

Stitch any darts.

Matching edges, place the wrong side of the stretch lace against the right side of the upper edge of the Back, using a 1:1 ratio.

Repeat for the upper edge of the Front, easing or folding the lace at the strap points and using a 1:1 ratio.

❖

Using a narrow zigzag, stitch along the inner edge of the lace as illustrated, stretching the lace slightly as you sew.

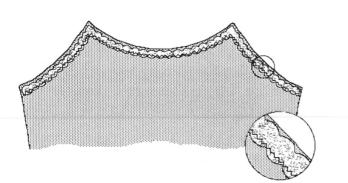

Trim the fabric under the lace close to the stitching.

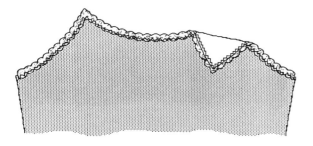

Stitch one side seam. To hem, choose lace (see pages 121–122) or finish with a pretty machine shell stitch finish (see page 38). I prefer flat lace stitched to the lower edge for a slip because it does not create a bump that can show through on your garment.

Stitch the remaining side seam, matching the lace at the upper and lower edges.

ADDING STRAPS

For spaghetti straps, use any of the specialized ready-made strap products on the market or follow the instructions below, using a loop turner.

Cut the straps to the length you need by 1½" (3.8 cm) wide. With right sides together, fold each strap in half lengthwise. Begin stitching at the outer edge and angle to ¼" (0.6 cm) from the folded edge as illustrated, creating a "funnel" for ease in turning. Continue stitching with a ¼" (0.6 cm) seam allowance to the other end. Trim the seam allowance.

Insert a loop turner through the narrow end of the strap and hook the fabric.

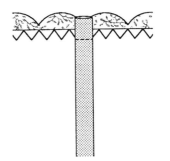

Pull the strap right side out. Pin the straps to the wrong side of the Back. Stitch across the strap ¼" (0.6 cm) from the upper edge.

Trim the strap close to the stitching.

Fold the strap up, enclosing cut edge. Bar-tack at the upper edge to secure.

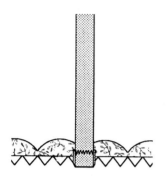

Try on the garment and adjust the strap to the finished length. Pin the front end of the strap in place on the Front. Stitch, using the same procedures as for the Back.

Half -Slip

This basic half-slip can be finished in many ways.

❖

To sew the half-slip, sew the side seams, then apply elastic or stretch lace to the waist as described on pages 110–114.

To hem, choose lace finish (see pages 121–122) or a pretty machine shell-stitch finish (see page 38). I prefer flat lace stitched to the lower edge of a slip because it does not create a bump that can show through on your garment.

Decorative Lace Touches

Lace and lingerie go hand in hand. Lace adds elegance to your garment and is surprisingly easy to work with.

Indulge yourself in the beautiful details of lace. Whether you use it on necklines or hemlines, lace makes any garment special.

Here are some tips for sewing with lace and also some ideas for how you can add touches of lace to any lingerie garment.

TIPS FOR SEWING WITH LACE

- When applying lace by a topstitching method, sew with a narrow zigzag or a straight stitch along the edge of the lace. If you are working with a rigid scalloped lace, you may want to stitch following the contours of the lace.

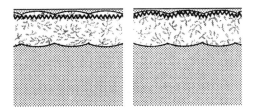

- For some garments, you might want to use a glue stick instead of pins to hold the lace in place for stitching.

- For gathered lace, either purchase pregathered lace trim in a variety of widths and styles, or gather your own, following these instructions. Purchase flat lace trim 2 to 3 times your finished hem measurement. Machine baste close to the straight edge. If the lace is 2 ½" (6.4 cm) wide or wider, baste two rows of gathering stitches ⅛" (0.3 cm) apart. Divide the lace and garment into fourths or eighths. Matching the divisions, pin the lace to the garment. Pull the basting threads to gather between the divisions.

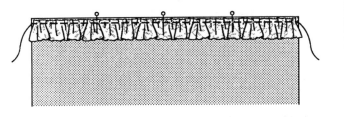

LACE HEM

Lace-trimmed hems are an easy, elegant way to finish your lingerie. This method works for both rigid and stretch lace.

Sew one garment side seam. Pin the lace along the hem edge with the wrong side of the lace against the right side of the gown, matching the lower edges.

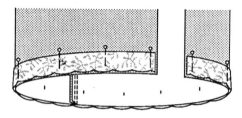

Using a straight or narrow zigzag stitch, sew the lace to the garment along the upper edge of the lace.

Trim the fabric behind the lace close to the stitching.

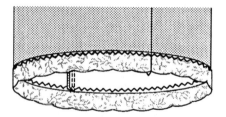

Stitch the remaining side seam, beginning at the lower edge of the lace.

LACE OVERLAY HEM

Let the lingerie fabric peek through your lace. This method works for both rigid and stretch lace.

Sew one garment side seam. With right sides up, pin the lace even with the lower edge. Trim the excess ends of the lace.

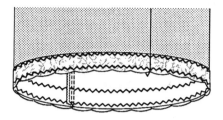

Stitch along the upper edge of the lace with a straight or narrow zigzag stitch. Zigzag again ¼" (0.6 cm) from the lower edge of the lace.

Trim away the fabric below the second stitching so that the edge of the lace conceals the cut edge of the fabric.

Beginning at the lower edge, stitch the remaining side seam.

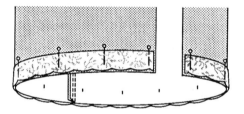

FLATLOCK LACE APPLICATION

The flatlock stitch on the serger is perfect for elastic and lace applications. Using two or three threads, it produces the smooth finish you find on expensive ready-to-wear lingerie. You use only two or three threads to do the flatlock stitch so that the lace will lie flat.

Set your serger for a flatlock stitch, following your owner's manual.

Pin right sides together and, using a long stitch length, stitch a narrow seam.

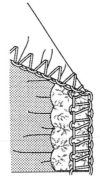

Once you have completed the stitching, pull the fabric and lace apart so that the seam flattens out and a trellis of stitches shows on the right side of the fabric.

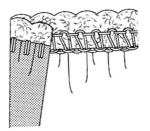

A Final Word

I hope you enjoy using the techniques in this book as much as I've enjoyed sharing them with you. These are my favorite short cuts and special secrets for sewing on knits. I hope I've helped you turn sewing into a fun, easy, and creative endeavor. Enjoy your success, have fun, and keep sewing!

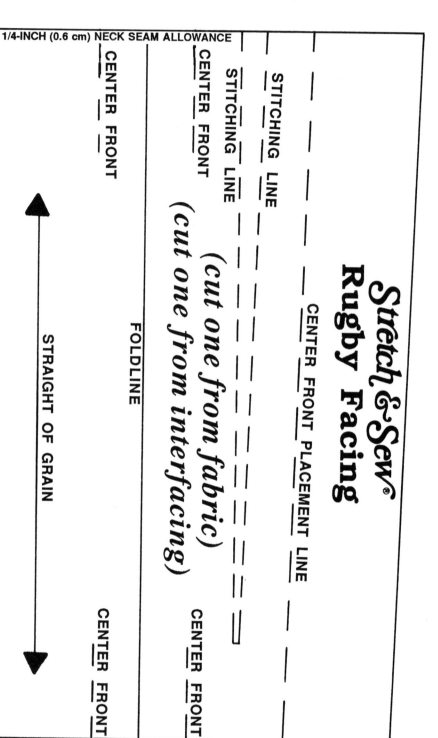

1/4-INCH (0.6 cm) NECK SEAM ALLOWANCE

CENTER FRONT

CENTER FRONT

STITCHING LINE

STITCHING LINE

CENTER FRONT PLACEMENT LINE

Stretch & Sew®
Rugby Facing

(cut one from fabric)

(cut one from interfacing)

FOLDLINE

STRAIGHT OF GRAIN

CENTER FRONT

CENTER FRONT

CENTER FRONT

INDEX

❖

❖

❖

❖